The
MASKQUERADE

DR. JENNIFER HOGUE

The Maskquerade

Trilogy Christian Publishers

A Wholly Owned Subsidiary of Trinity Broadcasting Network

2442 Michelle Drive, Tustin, CA 92780

For information, address Trilogy Christian Publishing

Rights Department, 2442 Michelle Drive, Tustin, Ca 92780.

Trilogy Christian Publishing/ TBN and colophon are trademarks of Trinity Broadcasting Network.

For information about special discounts for bulk purchases, please contact Trilogy Christian Publishing.

Trilogy Disclaimer: The views and content expressed in this book are those of the author and may not necessarily reflect the views and doctrine of Trilogy Christian Publishing or the Trinity Broadcasting Network.

10 9 8 7 6 5 4 3 2 1

Library of Congress Cataloging-in-Publication Data is available.

ISBN 979-8-89333-606-1

ISBN 979-8-89333-607-8 (ebook)

DEDICATION

To Sam, Nathan, Brayton, and Jordan, the physical manifestation of the deepest love, I know this side of heaven other than Christ in us the hope of glory. May we always search for God's truth in His Word, which will keep us free. May we dedicate our lives to help others live with the power of The Holy Spirit through Christ Jesus our Savior. May the five of us always stay in a posture of prayer, humility, and forgiveness, praising Him and walking for Him until we meet Him in heaven.

TABLE OF CONTENTS

PROLOGUE: AN INTERVIEW WITH THE DEVIL

"I have heard your prayer and seen your tears; I will heal you..."

(2 Kings 20:5, NLT)

I accepted Jesus as my Savior when I was a teenager. Are you ready for a shocker? Here it is: In my free will, I still proceeded to pick up a variety of serious "issues," including alcohol use, depression, anxiety, panic disorder, eating disorders, religious pride, shopping to excess, and divorce. There are more, but there is no need to list them all, and all of them are rooted in fear.

Although I wanted to do right, I could not seem to choose the path that would heal the pain. Instead, I chose to numb the pain with devices that kept me on the wrong road. I welcomed God into my territory, not realizing I needed to step into His Kingdom.

Surrounding me was a confederacy of people who did not walk with Him. I had no foundation on which to build and no builders to assist my growth in Christ. Often, when this is the case, the devil wins for a time.

In a moment, I will share with you an example of a typical day in my late teens and early twenties (sadly enough, those years were a cakewalk compared to my early thirties). While this story is real, I choose to portray certain details of my interview with the devil figuratively. But, yes, I did wear a crown all day long. It was a juxtaposition of my adolescent mask of darkness.

A Day in the Life

On this typical day, I woke up aware that dehydration had set in overnight. I could feel the deficiency making me sick. My sour stomach also ached from the overbearing emptiness caused by guilt over my addiction and actions. The emptiness even overpowered my hangover. The pain was unbearable. My head throbbed, and my eyes closed at the slightest sound. My tongue was stuck to the roof of my mouth. I had been drinking heavily the night before. When I drank, I drank all night and consumed as much alcohol as possible. That is just how I thought drinking worked.

I gazed up through the sparkly, prismatic crystals set in my tiara. The crown had slid down onto my face while I slept. I strained to focus my eyes on the bumper sticker I had attached to one of the blades on my ceiling fan. My father kept asking me to stop sticking things onto his house and cars. I liked bumper stickers and found them quite revealing. On this day, when I was the only thing in the room that was spinning, I kept thinking how can someone buy a staircase to heaven? It wouldn't be long before I understood that parabolic reference. I always pictured the woman in the Led Zeppelin song as some kind of princess. With only a word, she owned all her heart's desires. No pain, no fear, no lack—she had everything. I was trying to mimic her by manufacturing a stairway to heaven. My purpose was to find pleasure, but pleasure was hard to come by. I wondered why I was not like the woman in the song. Why did I have to hurt all the time? Why were my days devoted to finding ways to make the pain go away?

Dazed, I stared at the fan blade, singing the song in my head. For some reason, changing the road we are on kept coming to mind, like there are two roads we can take, but we can still always change the one we're on.

I did not believe this statement at all. I misunderstood my situation and thought that I was trapped in my pain. Consequently, I stayed there too long.

As I lay there that day, I thought, *Regardless of their biblical knowledge, whoever penned this song had great wisdom tucked away in the lyrics.*

I began to hum and realized that the song talks about a piper: To me, that piper was Jesus, and He was calling us to join Him. I had ignored His call for so long that I was surprised that my body was not yet in a coffin six feet underground, awaiting the judgment.

THE MASKQUERADE

As I read the bumper sticker on this particular morning, I felt more like a failure than a mask remover. I knew I was on the wrong road, but I did not know how to get on the right one. I did not know how to follow Jesus. My proclamation of accepting Christ had not led to my walking in a godly procession with His other saints. In fact, I was unsure whether I wanted to march for Christ all the time. How could He lead me home? I would have to give up and change so much. How was I even worthy? I had gone too far. I was too broken.

My hangover was awful, but before my feet hit the floor, I was already planning my next drink. I removed the crown from my brow, gently set it on the side table, and traded it for my smokes. When I was sober, nicotine made me more nervous than usual, but I smoked anyway. I opened my pill bottle and took two or three sedatives to steady my nerves and calm the fear and guilt.

I began to plan the rest of my day: I would shop all day and starve myself until dusk. Then, I would start the revelry all over again. I stepped out of my bed, remembering how I had drunk and drugged throughout the previous night and early dawn hours at my favorite club, The Masquerade. As I reminisced, I stooped to pick up my shoes from the floor. Reaching for the side table to stabilize myself, I inadvertently pressed my hand into the points of my crown. Feeling the pain, I lifted my hand and peeled the headdress from my squashed flesh. I placed the crown back on my head, smashed my half-smoked cigarette in the ashtray, and cursed the hurt. (In case you are wondering, tiaras, nose rings, tattoos, dark makeup, blue hair, and even full costume dresses were normal in my circles, whether day or night.)

Having steadied myself against the hallway wall, I made my way into the kitchen. I felt the sting of glass penetrating my heel as my feet hit the kitchen floor. My head was numb, but my face winced at the pain. Not that pain was anything new; I lived in pain. I wanted to believe that I wandered into it most days, but it was too obvious that I was choosing the torment and, ironically, always wondering, *Why do I feel this emptiness deep inside?*

Juggling my thoughts, I began to sing again. The lyrics rang true as I noticed a broken window and dried blood all over the tree and sidewalk just outside. I remembered that friends had come back to my house, done some cocaine, and gotten into a verbal altercation. The argument quickly became physical. Someone had a knife, and someone used it. The sad part is that I did not care at the time. I had not even paid attention to the fact that someone had been stabbed.

As I pulled the glass from my foot, I realized it did not hurt a bit; the sedative had begun to kick in. Remembering that I had a job interview at The Masquerade, I reached up to remove my crown. Then I realized that, at a club as weird as The Masquerade, my tiara would probably improve my chances of being hired. I left my crown on my head and prepared to return to the club, where I would fill out all the forms and interview for the job.

Little did I know, as my foot bled all over the floor, that I was planning more pain for myself. It was a mistake to apply for a job in a club I should never have even visited. Since I had numbed myself to reason, I was now ready for more things unreasonable. Isaiah's words had not yet penetrated my heart: "'Come now, let us reason together,' says the Lord. 'Though your sins are like scarlet, they shall be as white as snow; though they are red as crimson, they shall be like wool'" (Isaiah 1:18, NKJV).

My sins were still red.

I cleaned up the glass, wrapped up my foot, and headed back to the nightclub. I had to see whether my friends could help establish a reason for me to be at The Masquerade every day. Knowing I was late, I drove ninety miles per hour on the highway into downtown Atlanta. I even passed the college that I had just quit attending.

On this typical day, I was dazed on pills. I wore my tiara, all-black attire, and platform shoes. I smoked and listened to Led Zeppelin, still glazed over from leftover alcohol and tranquilizers. Somehow, I exited the highway safely, made it through the city, and turned into the club's parking lot.

As I opened my car door, I grabbed a pen and my purse. Before locking the car, I squeezed my pack of cigarettes to make sure I had an ample supply. I heard the rumble of a passing train echo through the mill equipment that was attached to the side of the warehouse that housed the bar. Meanwhile, small groups of people shuffled around behind the nightclub. I recognized the roadies from the night before; they were cleaning the equipment belonging to the rock band that had played.

Even in broad daylight, The Masquerade felt like an evil place. The freestanding building sitting on the outer edge of Atlanta looked like a deceptive gift from the devil lying on the Christmas tree skirt surrounding the city. From the warehouse area, I always noticed the buildings gathered together like a bundle of iron in the distance. The club was in a quiet, eerie district that most of society avoided.

With my dehydration now seeping through my temporary pill fix, I began to feel ill. I started to panic and searched my purse for another bitter comforter.

I entered the building by a side door of the gravel parking lot that held one of the two cars I was looking for. Inside, the club flaunted twenty-foot metal doors, wooden beams, and high ceilings. I walked through the smoky haze of the bar, guided by the red glow of the exit signs. I grabbed a glass from behind the first bar and shot soda water into it to swallow my remedy.

My stomach ached. I could find temporary peace in my pills, alcohol, cigarettes, shopping, starvation, and the attention of others. Still, I wondered why I was the only person who hurt this bad. I wanted to know why my shadow of emptiness felt larger than my soul.

Sunlight pushed through the cracked doorframe. Leaving the rays behind, I went deeper into the darkness. The club had three levels. The Masquerade had titled them "Hell," "Purgatory," and "Heaven." They counterfeited God's terms.

The friends I was looking for were most likely in the bar area called "Heaven." *Our world so often relates the word heaven to anything that satisfies our flesh,* I thought, as I remembered the song even mentioning something about words having two separate meanings.

"Hell" was empty, and "Purgatory" was closed. As I ascended the creaky, wooden stairs to "Heaven," I realized a small stream of sunlight had somehow found its way into the dark box. The fluorescent lights attached to the ceiling, some twenty feet above, led me up the stairs. Atop the stairs, a hidden door stood ajar, revealing the origin of the small stream of light. The sign on the door read "Office," so I entered. Sitting behind a large mahogany desk was an even larger albino man with pure white hair and long fingernails. He hissed as I entered.

I was feeling ill from all the substances, smells, and lack of anything good in or around me. Muttering, "Excuse me," I turned and ran to the restroom, which was directly across the hall.

As I ran in, my foot slipped into a puddle of water in front of the commode. As I caught myself, my tiara fell and tumbled behind a trash can. Barely making it to the toilet on time, I vomited and began crying aloud.

Once I collected myself, I stood up, left the stall, and reached behind the trashcan. I grabbed my tiara, placed it atop my head, and turned the corner to exit while simultaneously glancing into the mirror to check my face. To my horror, a cockroach was caught between the crystals in my crown! It was half-dead, half-alive, and flailing desperately.

I froze, unable to even lift my hand and remove the headdress. There, in the quasi-darkness, I looked like a mess. In fact, I was a masked hypocrite. My drunkenness, drug addiction, depression, fear, idolatry, and gluttony all screamed, "Nasty, rotten, hedonistic hypocrite!"

I pulled air into my lungs with a deep breath and swallowed hard. I removed the tiara, threw it into the gloom under the stall, and then shivered the tingles away. I heard my crown roll along the wood floor and eventually fall down into something as I left the room. The hollow thuds sounded like aluminum sheet metal in an open-air vent. I wondered if the roach was still intact.

I stepped back into the albino's office, my skin still crawling as I thought about the roach. I did not like roaches. I had a history with them, and it was not good.

"I'm sorry. I feel sick—dizzy—I'm here to apply for a full-time position. My friends are here somewhere," I said, stammering. I was about to cry, but I would not allow a tear to fall.

He reached out, his nails so long they almost curled, and handed me a white piece of paper. I knew I should not have accepted, but I did. I succumbed to the weakness Paul described in Romans 7:19 (NIV): "For I do not do the good I want to do, but the evil I do not want to do—this I keep on doing."

In the moment that I received the application, I could see into the albino man's eyes and realized that a color would have muddled the message they conveyed. His eyes spoke of the acceptance of alcohol, drugs, defective body image, endless gluttony, vanity, illusions of fame and idolatry.

I did not respond with words, but my actions expressed my agreement to accept the job. I stood there, noticing his pulse as the blood danced with his words. I had my eyes on the wrong person's blood. I suddenly felt like there were angels around me. They were humming but never pushed me or prodded me. They never exposed me to any images, but the albino did. I was veiled to the truth because of my choices giving ample room for evil persuasion.

The angels had joined me in the grossest place on earth so I would know that there was no secret too dark for them to help me reveal. They did only the Lord's bidding. My eyes kept searching the room, but I decided not to look to the angels, knowing they would not cross my will. I kept track of the light and noticed that the humming sound accompanied it.

In this instance, the angels relied on my heart and my hearing to function. Unfortunately, my heart was hard, and I was deaf to God's call. Even so, He never gave up on me. When I finally chose His path years later, I heard and reacted to the angels' praise. Their humming became audible: "Holy, holy, holy is the Lord God Almighty."

That day in the albino's office, I stood at the crossroads of two kingdoms and entertained the signals of both. What a double-minded woman, unstable in all her ways...

And no wonder, for satan himself masquerades as an angel of light. It is not surprising, then, if his servants masquerade as servants of righteousness. Their end will be what their actions deserve (2 Corinthians 11:14).

Never Too Late

The masquerade serves as a metaphor for my journey to healing. It illustrates my choice to travel the albino's fictitious steps in his deceptive world. I would remain trapped in that paradigm for more than eighteen years, believing a lie to avoid more pain or fear. On a symbolic level, I eventually chose to step out of that room in order to step into healing in the Kingdom of God.

It took some time before I realized that we are all in a masquerade on some level and at some point in our lives. This is the place where we are deceived, whether we live in denial of our sinful ways or flat-out revel in iniquity. When we recognize the maskquerade, admit our pain, and give it up to God, we step into healing that portion of our hearts.

Every time we choose evil over the ways of God, we allow satan to employ us for his purposes. However, we are always free to leave his maskquerade. Isaiah prophesied to Hezekiah when his end was near: "I have heard your prayer and seen your tears; I will heal you. On the third day from now you will go up to the temple of the LORD" (2 Kings 20:5, NIV).

God gave me a third day and freed me from the bondage of tremendous pain and torment by simply allowing the Holy Spirit to guide me to the heavenly Jerusalem.

Nothing—absolutely nothing—is impossible for God (Matthew 19:26).

I am sharing my testimony with you. I felt wrecked, overwhelmed, and trapped. What I discovered is this: He has grace for us all, anytime and all the time. You can never say too much time has passed. How do I know? Because He fixes all of the pain that I give Him because it's part of life. Today, I am healthy, peaceful, and blessed. He has healed me and is healing me daily. Now, I have the peace of constant hope and the victory of true healing.

For too long, I decided to stay. In fact, I was downright terrified and confused. I didn't know how not to stay. I did not even know I was wearing yet another mask to mask the fear. Although there had been many reasons for me to step onto the wrong path, none of them forced me to stay. I was choosing the lie!

The Piper—the living God—is always leading His people into the deeper reasons guiding our choices for pain so that we can heal from them as we journey. His forgiveness is available, as Isaiah 1:18 attests.

I learned that through life if I just simply recognize the pain and accept that I make the choice to let go, He will heal me. Follow Him is what I learned!

CHAPTER ONE

LEAVE BEHIND THE MASKQUERADE OF PAIN

STEP ONE: OUT OF DENIAL AND INTO HOPE

"Heal me, LORD, and I will be healed; save me and I will be saved, for you are the one I praise"

(Jeremiah 17:14, NIV)

Picture a big castle where you are attending a maskquerade ball, even if you are bawling your eyes out right now in fear or pain. Dressed in royal attire, you know once you ascend the stairs outside, you will enter a marble entry with multiple fingerlings of hallways jutting off in numerous directions adorned with crystal chandeliers. All encompassed from above by two huge surrounding spiral staircases. You can go up two different ways or explore the lower level first.

However, one thing you can be sure of: As long as you keep your mask on, no one will know who you are or how to track your decisions and location in order to help you. You can even think you are hiding from God like Gideon, David, Elijah, Adam, Eve; this list goes on... He loves you, sees you, and is just waiting for you to reach out to Him.

Only God can see the heart. We can only see the mask others choose to show us at any given time. Others can only see the mask we are willing to present at any given time. That is powerful, and that should be carefully thought about; you could miss a lot with a mask on. In fact, most block your peripheral completely.

Think back to the rooms that you have traveled through. Some rooms bring back good memories; some bring back bad ones. You might remember a hospital room in which you heard and saw your child for the first time. You might also remember a hospital room in which you left a piece of your heart when a loved one passed away. How about a courtroom that felt like it took your soul?

Do you remember a bedroom in which you felt safe? Or a bedroom where you lost something you feel you can never recover? Do you see a dark room where you were deeply hurt or broken? A room in which you felt the pain would never end? Perhaps it was a classroom where you were ridiculed and belittled. Or maybe you left your heart in the kitchen where your spouse told you about the other love in their life? Is a piece of your heart still held in a courtroom, a classroom, a church room, a prison cell, a sanctuary, a playground, a bathroom, an office?

Is there a room that has walled in your fear, heartache, tears, and ultimately your heart, or part of your heart? Think about it: Is there even a mask powerful enough to cover the pain? Allow your heart to be open and soft so that you can eventually allow God to repossess all those parts and heal you. Begin to establish the habit of letting His truth come into your heart to counterattack the lies that keep you wanting to cover them. Psalm 147:3 (NIV) reads, "He heals the brokenhearted and binds up their wounds."

We have to face the pain, with Christ's help, in order to discover what led us into our maskquerade, to begin with. I think of people in actual prisons or foreign countries in bondage and wonder what they go through. Yet, there are other kinds of entrapments. I decided to stay trapped in an unhealthy marriage for way too long. I allowed the fear of the legal battle to control my life for years. Our world, others, even friends, media, and society try to imprison us daily with lies about who we are, who God is, and what we are supposed to do and be.

Do you feel scared or trapped? If so, in what way are you willing to let God help you out? Do you believe He really will? Is the fear going to command your destiny, or will you let the light in, move on, and remove the mask?

A Step Toward Freedom

In my early thirties, when I finally decided to give God my whole heart, He led me up a stairway to heaven. He took me out of what I thought was permanent entrapment in the maskquerade of pain; He drew me out of my territory and into an enduring healing in His Kingdom. He did it again at thirty-nine and again at forty-nine. Now, these particular ages above were big moments, but believe me, it is a daily reprieve.

Prayerfully, I will always stay humble, faithful, and pliant to His Word, His ways. Why? Because we are a constant work in progress, and He is always there to forgive and help when we allow Him to heal us. We are sinful creatures that crave our own fleshly desires, but God also allows us a choice as free-will agents, and He is a gentleman. The stairway to our flesh or the stairway to His Spirit (Galatians 6:8).

It all began with my first step, which was to allow God to reveal the mask of denial that kept me bound at that moment. When I stopped denying my co-dependent nature at thirty-nine years old, my belief in the seeming impossibility of being trapped in a horrible marriage, suddenly my overwhelming fear was replaced with the hope/awareness that there had to be something better.

He tells us in Romans 5:3–5 that even to get to hope, we must first suffer and allow that suffering to produce in us perseverance, then perseverance into a new character, and that results in our ability to hope. But don't disregard Romans 5:5 (NIV), "Hope doesn't put us to shame." Our sin does, though, and a lot of shame. Also, the powerhouse that we will delve into wholeheartedly in multiplicity: "Because God's love has been poured out into our hearts through the Holy Spirit who has been given to us."

Please, trust me, it was a grueling circular process where I would try and fail over and over, not realizing that I wasn't trusting the perseverance in order to change my character from fear to faith-based. It was a process, and during some seasons in my life, the process felt like an unbearably long series of never-ending battles, inclusive of great losses that felt close to complete defeat. The darkness seemed like it would never lift, and the mask felt glued to my face.

An example prior to thirty-nine was a step towards internal freedom around age thirty-three in my life. I remember leaving behind the scorching Mississippi heat to enter the building where a portion of my healing unknowingly would begin. The cool, white hallway led me to a safe place to heal, a place where I felt at ease. A single lamp stand illuminated my footsteps as I entered the serene room. I was the first person to arrive at the treatment center that day. Regardless of my fear, the accomplishment of having shown up made me feel good, at least for a moment.

I scanned the room, admiring its simplicity. The only furnishings were the lamp and nine velvet armchairs arranged in a circle. I pictured myself sinking into the down-filled cushions and disappearing inside them. Although I felt safe upon entering the room, my heart now felt as though it were in a vice grip. Somehow, I was thankful for the clutch that kept my softening heart from pounding out of my chest.

My eyes leaked. I had to look up to balance the tears inside my lower lids, hoping they would evaporate before falling. By this time, I was okay with crying but still a little hesitant. My breath was hard to pull in and let out. I felt dizzy from the lack of oxygen. Yet I was thankful for the soft room because I believed that I really belonged in a hard iron and concrete jail cell.

God allowed part of my heart to be healed in that quiet room. It was the part I gave Him on that first step. Having finally decided to come down from the devil's staircase and leave the maskquerade behind, I found the angels waiting for me with open arms. I still feared the unknown, but the fear had become a kind of willing trepidation.

Accepting the dread of the unknown was a significant step in my healing. God took the sickness in my life, and with each step toward Him, He healed me—right before my eyes. As I persevered, I could see the next step, and my character was slowly changing and letting hope in.

You may be feeling the same dread right now. You might feel numb, unsure, and scared. These feelings are normal; accept them. Healing is not comfortable. That is why so many stay sick. I repeat this truth often: If I leave my false comfort and heal, I will step into the place of true comfort much faster than if I stay in my pain.

You will be okay if you trust Christ. Embrace the pain so that you can overcome it. Trust me, there were times I felt like I was freefalling into hell, but I never hit the ground. He always caught me on an eagle's wing. Sometimes, inches before my demise, I felt His grip, but that is the faith part, the part that inevitably makes you better.

The Rooms

We will walk together through many rooms; a few examples briefly: the room at the treatment center was my transition room out of the maskquerade of some of my persistent sinful ways. Do you remember the rooms of your pain or out of your pain?

The courtroom that allowed me freedom from years of pain was precious until that courtroom took my children for a time, senselessly, causing them some of the worst pain they would ever have to endure. In fact, I decided to put my mask back on because watching them hurt, hurt worse than any pain I had ever felt prior. But this is the cycle of life; we have challenges and suffering in this life. We do not arrive until He calls us home. However, we can allow these stairs to destroy us or to propel us forward and upward.

When we accept Christ, we also have to accept the fact that our sinful nature will always beckon us back to the wrong path. Do you see where this has happened to you? To combat this relentless lure, we need healing and then training in righteousness. Unfortunately, my only training prior to thirty-three was in worldliness.

What has your training been? What about the opposite, too much "religious" training? Not God's intention but man's imposition that made you feel incapable of righteousness.

Another room I will never forget is the space in which I received salvation. As a young teenager, I accepted Christ into my broken heart at a friend's house. In John 14:6 (NKJV), Jesus said, "I am the way and the truth and the life. No one comes to the Father except through Me." Salvation comes through Christ.

I always felt a strong call from the Lord. I fought through the worldly web satan had woven around me by getting as much of Jesus as possible through my friends and friends' parents. As soon as I would get home to my room, the devil would steal any godly seed I had received. I kept trying to do right but just could not live up to the standard I desired and deemed necessary. Do you see this conundrum in your life, a counterattack against whatever is good? I call this "the Romans 7 syndrome."

My room as a teenager was a suite suited for a queen. The chamber sat atop three stories of bay windows that mimicked a castle tower. To get to my abode, I had to step four flights up a staircase adorned with pink shag carpet; we must remember this was in the 1980s. The space was beautifully decorated, but beneath the surface, it was infested with roaches; some were actual insects, but most were spiritual "bugs." We will talk more about my teenage years and the above rooms as we journey.

We will also visit another room along the stairway—the room that allowed me to understand how to comfort all the hurt along the way. It was just like the room in Damascus where Ananias laid his hands on Paul, and the apostle's life was transformed (Acts 9:15–18).

Addiction Denial

The addiction and fear I suffered were my way of escaping pain. When I was hurting, I would consume a lot of beer, some liquor or wine, and sometimes packs of cigarettes. Many times, I tried to mask the fear, depression, and guilt with more medicine than necessary.

For the majority of that time, I gossiped to friends about my troubles and desperately attempted to get their agreement with no plans to change out of pure fear. I used this technique to comfort, excuse, sustain, and justify my behavior. We all do it, but we need to remember Job and keep our mouths shut while the parabolic Bildad, Eliphaz, and Zophar are rambling. We may even be playing these roles ourselves.

My "pain management" tactics were unhelpful; days like the ones I have described always ended in severe shame and hopelessness.

Emotionalism

Emotions stem from deeper issues. Pain and fear were the catalysts for my emotions. I used them as a faulty coping mechanism. Severe anxiety attacks soon manifested as agoraphobia. I could not leave my house. Crowds and busy places terrified me. I stayed depressed and full of apprehension all day long; I was imprisoned in my mind, my first marriage, and my home.

These issues made me angry, bitter, and frustrated. My pain caused me to feel estranged and different from everyone else. The panic trapped me in isolation. I, in turn, used seclusion to "treat" my sense of estrangement. That is not unusual; we often use pain to fix pain. When COVID-19 hit, I was suddenly allowed to actually wear a mask everywhere, and in my flesh, it felt like an old friend.

Controlled by Consequences

Instead of being fearful, intoxicated, and hurting, I wanted to be "normal." I desired to live the "normal" life everyone except me seemed to be living. I wanted to be free of consequences like speeding or worse tickets, medicine for fear, daily arguments with a contentious partner, abuse, court, pain, and sadness. Being sober, peaceful, and healthy seemed impossible to me. Early on in life, I added fuel to the fire of my difficulties by making poor decisions from an inebriated mindset. The cycle kept going.

My desperate need to fix myself resulted in me allowing the world to influence me and shifted me into thinking I was somehow in control. When we try to control what God intends to control, we are out of control. My chain of command was upside down, with me at the top. It resembled more of a shackle with a ball attached. I put the fetter on with the devil's help. My mind was the ball weighing the manacle in place.

Faulty Body Image

I starved myself on occasion, threw up, and sometimes took pills to stay thin. First thing each morning, I determined the path of my day based on the digits displayed on the scale. I began to realize that math and eating disorders are tightly intertwined. The figures on the scale, the tags on the clothes, the measuring tape, the body fat percentage, the reps required, the miles to run, and the number of bites I would allow or disallow—these were just a few of the issues I struggled with daily. Can you relate?

To Struggle Is Human

We are human. We have struggles, issues, pain, and sad days. What is not normal is for us to cycle in defeat and pain daily. Christ overcame on our behalf. He recognizes our helplessness and intends for us to tap into His healing power.

God finds no dark corner too horrible for His Spirit to enter and pull us out. My corner was fear, worthlessness, and victimization. He did not require any worth from me. He taught me that no one's pain is as great as that suffered by His Son, who came with gifts we could not earn. Shortly after He pulled me out, He impressed on me a gift of self-worth that surpassed my hopes and dreams; my worth was suddenly in Him. I became a victor, "a human victor," and by saying that, we must understand that life will bring us many trials and tribulations, but we must not lose hope because while our pain is not over, we must keep stepping with Him.

These steps into healing apply to all issues and all people. A healthy life may seem impossible now, but there is a way. At this moment, getting out of bed may be your first priority. That is okay. We can take this journey into healing one step at a time. We must only be willing to let God order our steps. He will give us the strength needed to take each step. The steps are there to use over and over as pain rises up. Never give up because as useless or hopeless as you may feel now, if you are still breathing, God still needs you!

A wise man once explained the difference between traveling up the staircase and down: If you are heading up the stairs and trip, you will most likely catch yourself. You might end up one or two stairs back if you descend at all. But if you stumble while traveling down the staircase, you are likely to land at the bottom with bruises and maybe some badly broken bones to show for it. A bit like the analogy of the club called The Masquerade from the prologue. The stairs went up to heaven from purgatory and down to hell.

We need to get on the right set of stairs and start climbing. The struggle upward is worthwhile. It leads to a state of healing described by Jeremiah: "Behold, [in the future restored Jerusalem] I will lay upon it health and healing, and I will cure them and will reveal to them the abundance of peace (prosperity, security, stability) and truth" (Jeremiah 33:6, AMP).

Our Pain Is Real

Most people are familiar with emotional hurts. The damage done to us or by us year after year causes us real pain. The hurt hardens parts of the heart and fragments parts of the soul. We carefully box up that portion, only to find that, instead of healing, the pain grows. Our issues are made evident by our anger, fear, insecurity, guilt, unbelief, bitterness, fear of abandonment, loneliness, and worry, all rooted in trauma. We cleave to worry even when Matthew 6:27 (BSB) asks, "Who of you by worrying can add a single hour to his life?"

We will eventually step into a place of hope. On this step, we will learn how to unmask the pain and release fear just like the widow at Zarephath did (1 Kings 17). She was facing death by starvation; she had a legitimate reason to respond in fear to Elijah's request for food. Instead, she stepped up to hope as God requested through His prophet. By taking that step, she learned about more than God's ability to produce a limitless supply. She also found faith, life (for herself and her son), and healing for the portion of her heart that she had boxed in with worry. Like the widow at Zarephath, we are journeying toward God's unfailing provision and healing.

The journey involves choices, some of which can prolong unnecessary suffering. When we refuse to let God make us whole, our distress is driven into addiction, depression, performance orientation, judgment, rebellion, idolatry, adultery, eating disorders, and more. The longer we refuse God, the deeper we delve into issues of fear, estrangement, allowing sexual and verbal abuse, rage, self-inflicted wounding, divorce, physical ailments, addiction, codependency, isolation, and idolatry.

Most pain stems from events and issues in our lives that got suppressed. As a result, we feel a nagging deficiency; we are unsure of the origin of our pain or the nature of the missing piece we seek. This bondage and confusion (or denial) is exactly where the enemy would like us to stay. He wants us to believe that we are trapped in a place of defeat, suffering on the devil's immobile stair.

To break the bondage means to look to God, as Psalm 65:2–3 (NLT) reveals, "For you answer our prayers. All of us must come to you. Though we are overwhelmed by our sins, you forgive them all."

We are about to take the initiative to leave the maskquerade of our pain behind for good. Our first step is to be without denial; we have to realize and accept the fact of our pain. We must admit it and trust God. We need to be wholeheartedly obedient to the healing process He laid out for us. We cannot quit after taking the first few steps and expect to experience the best outcomes of our lives on earth. We must climb with perseverance all the steps to healing. Let us commit to the stairway to God's heaven so we can experience blessed and complete lives.

It is easy to have a genuine desire for healing. It is common to get off to a great start. All too often, however, we give up, lose hope, slow down, or quit. Persistence and consistency are not automatic. I have found that without the fullness of God's Spirit, I am not consistent in anything but sin. Let us step into His Spirit and allow His Spirit to step into us. This is where healing begins. (We will learn how to do this through a combination of real-life examples and biblical exploration.)

Once we set our face like flint towards healing, as perseverance over pain begins to grow our character, we can step into the mindset of hope, which naturally leads us into the faith-filled place of healing. In your sadness, this might seem impossible, but all things are possible with God (Matthew 10:27). Philippians 4:13 (NIV) says, "I can do everything through him who gives me strength." We will step out of denial through intentional action and into hope.

We have to accept our God-ordained paths and not the faulty ones that lead us away from God. Jeremiah quoted God's command, "Stop at the crossroads and look around. Ask for the ancient, godly way, and walk in it. Travel its path, and you will find rest for your souls..." (Jeremiah 6:16, NLT)

Upward Steps

There are stairsteps into His Kingdom and out of the Maskquerade of cyclical fear and pretending. The same is true in the natural: the temple was elevated; each section rose higher than the rest. We will enter His gates with thanksgiving, His court, the court of women or the Gentile's court, with praise up into the holy place and then into the Holy of Holies. You can only arrive at the next level by steps. Each time we ascend in His purpose, we choose the right way: up, not down; forward, not backward; into healing and away from more sickness. It is important that we follow God's leading as Jeremiah explained: "I know, O Lord, that a man's life is not his own; it is not for man to direct his steps" (Jeremiah 10:23, NIV).

As we continue our upward trek, we will highlight certain truths allowing for a new awareness in each step of our journey. New awareness gives us revelation of the many facets/perspectives that will continually cast new rays of light. This awareness will serve to reveal new power and wisdom. They are symbols and guideposts for your upward course. They will direct you to the foot of the cross, where true strength is found. They will also remind you to step up and away from pain by allowing God to complete you through the blood of Christ. You will begin to see and hear things differently.

We are traveling together, and the stairs are safe. On each one, you will probably find several reminders of your past, how far you have come as well as how much you have changed and are changing. There are biblical reminders designed to ensure a lasting healing. It will help us to become more aware of His Scripture and more accustomed to practicing His truths and His ways.

By the grace of God, we are already free to make this choice. So why do we bolt ourselves into rooms filled with pain? Why do we shackle ourselves to the handrail on one step? Why do we stop on the bottom steps? I did this for decades in my first marriage, the fear of the divorce proceedings and the utter despair during the ten-year custody battle. However, it felt at times satan was winning the battles matters, not when it is God who always wins the war!

We live in the age of grace! We are at liberty to choose life. Are you willing to release your fear and remove your mask? Then, let the bolts be undone, and the doors opened. My beautiful friends, let the shackles fall and the true path be revealed. Allow Him to have your whole soul and soften your whole heart. Then, we mindfully step toward Him. When we permit God to work in us, the healing ensues.

The Deadbolt of Denial

Pain is not the catalyst for our bondage. Denial is the primary issue that blocks healing. Now, denial is many times smothered in fear, and we will cover this, I promise. It is, in fact, the deadbolt on the door of healing. Once we admit we want to leave the maskquerade where our pain has been kept... to climb the stairs leading to temple to receive our healing, we are on our way! We step out of denial by accepting our responsibility for the duration and depth of pain that we allowed and move in faith. We cannot heal if we cannot get the deadbolt undone. Ironically, all of us who have accepted Christ already have the key!

We have the key! If we fail to see the part we play in maintaining our pain, we will remain immersed in it. We control how pain affects us; we can stop the ache by accepting this fact.

This may be hard to recognize right now, but hold on to this truth. I am speaking of the fortitude that characterizes a victorious state. We can use this information as a springboard to get out and stay out of the pain. That is not to say that your life will be forever pain-free. Tribulation is inevitable as long as we live on this earth in emotional and fleshly bodies. The good news is that if you believe, God can heal you.

Denial is the blatant rejection of an obvious fault in our character. It is hard to come to terms with denial, but it is not impossible. This garment or mask we choose to wear is a cloak that seemingly conceals many sins. It whispers to us, saying that hiding and excusing our transgressions is okay. Denial tells us that we can use pride, bitterness, and anger to mask our fear and pain. The Bible tells us differently. It says that pride comes before destruction (Proverbs 16:18). It feeds denial's defiance.

The shroud of denial is heavy, but once we throw it off, we will experience tears of joy. The load of life will lighten because humility leads to blessing and honor. If denial is our blatant rejection of an obvious fault in our character, then we must preserve to trust that our pain will stay until we change our character and accept that we are fallible. Once this simple action occurs, our hope grows, and change is possible.

Revelation Bride

I felt incapable of coming out of my pain. I was sure I was stuck in it. Many times, we realize these insecurities during life-changing events: our college years, marriage, pregnancy, divorce, separation, a breakup, illness, sobering up, healing, the death of a loved one, or any other transitional situation. We allow life to overwhelm us with the sins of our past and the responsibilities of our unknown future. Sometimes, we need to be jolted out of going through our unhealthy motions.

Because I was so sick at the time, my first wedding was one of those jolts for me. Although I kept trying to keep on the mask of a bride and desperately wanted to be one, I was not; I was following suit or attempting to build a castle made of sand to place a white fence around, soon to crumble and leave me washed up on a scary, lonely shore. However, I was in complete denial and fear of this fact. I kept trying to make the outside prettier, hoping that the prettiness would eventually sink inside somehow.

A decade later, while watching my wedding video, the shiny jewel sparkling out of a white gold setting on my finger represented a covenant I was unaware existed. I knew the term "marriage" but had no idea of what God had intended it to represent. I didn't realize that it symbolized the divine relationship between Christ and the Church. The idea of an unconditional, eternal alliance with anyone or anything was beyond me. My hurt had caused me to become a skeptic, and the knowledge of the pain I was stepping into was real.

While watching my wedding video, I remembered the gardenias' sweet honeysuckle smell and the sound of James Taylor playing softly as my Jesus and I strolled onto the dance floor; He was still there in the center of it all regardless of my ignorant, faulty decision. I cannot regret this decision because my three beautiful children are here, and I have a testimony to help others out, and that will have to be worth the pain (Romans 8:28).

My tiara sparkled; my white dress flowed with the music. Regally postured wait staff poured bubbly champagne into crystal goblets. Not knowing I would soon have bruises and tears daily. There was laughter and children's crisp white clothes stained by splashes of Shirley Temple. The bridesmaids' ball gowns filled the room, swishing in the cool night air. Not knowing that soon I would be gasping for breath and freedom. The stage of the old rustic inn was set as though for worldly royalty. The scene gave the appearance of perfection. The appearance, however, was deceptive.

As I watched the video, I cried. I remembered all the hidden drugs, affairs, lies, deceit, mental instability, and manipulation. I was surrounded by so much horrible abuse, mental and physical, daily; the insecurity, the uncertainty, the inability, and the lack made me so insecure. I felt so unqualified to love, so sick inside with the fear of knowing I did not love myself. I was a wounded vessel—afraid, hurt, and filled with unbelief. How could I have even gotten married in denial of that much pain? How in the world can I get out?

I was married for way too long a time, and it was not ordained by God, thus ending in divorce. I have stepped a good distance from my wedding video and all of its hidden pain. My Jesus even provided me an earthly Kinsman Redeemer, reestablishing a true earthly marriage covenant for me, a blessing I never thought was possible. I am now ten years remarried, so please never give up hope!

This time, we left out the big dress, the hundreds of flowers, the crowd, and the feelings of insufficiency; we remembered Him with communion. We included the all-sufficient Jesus, our acceptance of each other's imperfection, our desire for constant healing, and the eternal unity of the agape love God intended us to have for one another. We were anointed and ordained to be together. Why the way it happened? Free will? Maybe God's will for His glory? All I know for sure is it is good now.

When we heal, not only do we get better, but our surroundings eventually do as well. Most times, the people around us will either follow suit or make their exit. Eventually, your healing encompasses you and spreads to those you allow God to love through you. I am not saying that others will definitely change just because we do. Many times, they don't.

If we truly change, however, we will see others much differently. We will be willing to step out on faith, not reside in fear. Our love will then lend itself to produce the same effect in those who are willing. We will not only become healed vessels; we will become healing vessels.

Room to Hold the Holy Spirit

It wasn't until many years after the tears fell and I recognized my pain watching the video that I was even ready to confront my defiance. Stepping out of denial in my early thirties was my first step into a radical life change. I allowed God to alter me, and I literally became a new creation. He did not change me all at once, but there was a specific moment in which healing began—a moment when transformation became my path: "And be not conformed to this world: but be ye transformed by the renewing of your mind, that ye may prove what *is* that good, and acceptable, and perfect, will of God" (Romans 12:2, KJV).

I would call the change a death of my flesh because almost everything about me began to change. Second Corinthians 5:17 (ESV) says, "Therefore, if anyone is in Christ, he is a new creation; the old has gone, the new has come!" God began to mold me into the image of Christ.

We cannot even begin to grasp the all-powerful capabilities of God. We rarely allow Him room to do the miraculous. His healing can exceed any and all of our expectations if we allow Him.

This transformation occurred around the Thanksgiving and Christmas holiday seasons. It came after I had surrendered my first marriage (or so I thought), definitely unnecessary substances, gone through treatment, and spent about six months in absolute sobriety and obedience to the Lord.

I felt like Esther in her period of preparation before she could go into the king. It was the season before she stepped into his court and received power: "He set a royal crown on her head" (Esther 2:17, NIV). She had to take some cleansing steps before she could make a request from the king. God cleans us out in order to fill us up.

The preparation served me well, but it was just the beginning of my cleansing. The day came when I walked into the church office, hesitant and irritated at having to step back into counseling so soon. Only four months had passed since my completion of a three-month period of intensive outpatient treatment. In my mind, I did not need this. I was sober and doing just fine. I was separated from the man who hurt me, estranged from my two children, working my fingers to the bone to make ends meet, and crying myself to sleep at night, but yep, just fine.

Despite my cynicism, this room would prove significant. In fact, of all the rooms I had passed through up to this point, the impact of this one was the most astonishing. My transformation was ignited in this very "Damascus room" of my own.

The passageway leading to this room had a bookshelf full of great Christian books. I began to scan the spines. I used my fingers to walk from book to book, reciting their titles as I went. My hand landed on *Christ in You*. The title made no sense to me, but it was about to be clarified. I had accepted Him as Savior, yet this phrase sounded strange. I tilted my head, shrugged my shoulders, and turned an unexpected corner in my life. Although I did not know it yet, Christ was about to step into me in a greater way.

That day, I walked into a room just like the room the apostle Paul entered in Damascus (Acts 9:17–18). I did not even know such a room existed. My Ananias was a woman named Vicki D. It may sound silly, but that is what I call her. I did not know such power of impartation existed. There was no reference point in my life for it.

What we are taught or not taught so often limits us and keeps us in bondage. I was in denial of the fullness of God's Holy Spirit. I did not deny the existence, but I did not understand how the Spirit could live within me. If you are unsure as I once was, my desire is to make certain that you leave this book understanding the availability of the Holy Spirit in all His fullness. We are going to take each step up, hand in hand, and I will explain these truths all the way up the stairs.

Here in this room, I received a healing that I was not aware was available; it was a healing I was sure I did not deserve. Yet, I emptied myself out enough to allow God to have all of me. That is the very beginning of our stairway: openness to God. It is the point at which the rubber tip of your shoe touches the baseboard below the first stair. It is the initiation of humility, the freedom to surrender in brokenness, and begins our journey into healing.

Vicki D. opened the conversation. "Jennifer, I am so glad you decided to show up. I told your husband I would not call you. He told me he hoped you would come." In other words, I had to reach out; that's just how God works most of the time.

Her voice was soft, and when I crossed the threshold of her office, I got dizzy. It was not the same kind of dizziness I experienced at the treatment center or from my nagging anxiety. Now, I was strong and physically healthy. I was dizzy because she carried the Spirit of the Lord within her in such capacity that His glory was overflowing all around her. I was love-struck by His Spirit and confounded, all at the same time.

I sat down and breathed deeply. I now knew how to combat anxiety with healthy methods, but this was not anxiety; this was new and mysterious. Even though my flesh was uncomfortable, I did not want to combat the unknown feeling. The most amazing thing, other than the obvious anointing or presence of God, was the love in her eyes. I had never seen anything like it. God in her was fascinating and comforting.

I knew the counseling systems well, so I cut through the small talk by getting straight to the significant part. "I am done, Vicki. I do not want to go back to that house or that marriage. But I miss my children, and I feel like I am doing to them what was done to me."

My voice cracked. Once again, I had to do the eyes-looking-up thing to try to dry up the tears.

"What does God want you to do?" She looked into my soul when she spoke. Her eyes had Christ so deeply embedded in them that it was difficult to think. She knew my passion for the Scriptures. In fact, she knew everything about me because it was not her but Christ in her counseling me. I could not be anything other than surrendered in His presence and hers. My attempt would have been futile and defeating.

"He wants me to trust Him and adhere to His covenants." I knew the answer, but knowing the answer is nothing unless you are willing to live it.

"What is covenant to you?"

I only knew the flat definition, so she explained with power from her Spirit. "Covenant is what God promised you when He told you all your sins would be forgiven as He sacrificed His own Son on the cross for you, all of them. You have a representation of that beautiful covenant on earth with your Jesus." She was soft, not an ounce of judgment in her voice.

A tear fell from my eye, and in that moment, something deep within me grabbed hold of that promise, that covenant, and out of sheer thanksgiving, I made a vow to surrender. With just a shred of hope that God would fix all the brokenness, I stepped out of my flesh, goals, plans, fears, insecurities, needs, wants, dreams, life. It was the last surrender at that moment, that last goodbye to my flesh, and she knew it.

"Hmm," she said.

At the end of this particular session, Vicki D. stood to her feet and asked, "Do you mind if I lay my hands on you and pray over you?" As she spoke, she walked around her desk slowly; she hummed and rubbed her hands together, her eyes closed in prayer.

"Sure," I said, weeping in my emptiness, surprised I breathed in a sweet aroma.

"Jennifer, God sees your obedience, and He will bless obedience. He knows your heart, and He honors those who honor Him, His ways, and His covenants."

She hummed again after speaking. Her voice was always soft and filled with the genuine authority of God.

"I know God has me in His hand," I said. "I can feel the weightlessness."

As I spoke these words, I believed who Christ was, but I did not yet have the ability to understand what He intended for my life because my sin and ignorance were keeping me veiled. We are not able to comprehend His ways without His Spirit. I was still in operation mode instead of flow mode (this point will become clear as our journey unfolds). In simple terms, I did not yet know what was meant by the words: "Christ in you, the hope of glory" (Colossians 1:27).

I lowered my head, closed my eyes, and had no idea that I was allowing myself, my flesh, to die. Vicki placed her hands on my head and began to pray for me. Her words went from recognizable ones into a language I could not interpret. My spirit, however, was familiar with every syllable. I began to cry with no effort on my part. My tears dropped so fast and hard they splashed upward as they plinked off the thin pages of my Bible, which was open on my lap.

Vicki D. asked God to protect me and not let me be like Lot's wife. I had just privately studied that account the night before. She was praying for me, standing in the gap created by my lack of understanding. While I had followed the Lord's guidance to read that passage of Scripture, I had not yet known what to pray for.

She prayed in her prayer language for a while. In the midst of it came a discernible voice in English, "Jennifer, My beautiful daughter, welcome home. I have been calling you since I gave you ears to listen. Stay on My narrow path; each step will lead you closer to Me."

It was God's voice through Vicki D. I felt a rush of wind and warmth. In that moment, God allowed me to understand His fullness, the concept of Christ in me for eternity.

The Seal of Renewal

We will explain this fullness as we travel up the staircase. I can tell you now that this power has made healing possible for me. What I received from God that day was the baptism of the Holy Spirit or the fullness of the Holy Spirit.

You may have already experienced the fullness in your own life, and praise God; if not, keep stepping because we are going to grab hold of this powerful truth. Luke explains this baptism in the Book of Acts:

Suddenly a sound like the blowing of a violent wind came from heaven and filled the whole house where they were sitting. They saw what seemed to be tongues of fire that separated and came to rest on each of them. All of them were filled with the Holy Spirit and began to speak in other tongues as the Spirit enabled them.

Acts 2:2–4

From the examples I just shared in my session with Vicki D., you may have a fair sense of this promise. Or you may need more explanation and guidance. We will be diligent to cover this truth so that you and every reader will receive the teaching that is necessary to healing. Revelatory learning is imperative for the permanence of our healing.

He saved us not because of the righteous things we had done but because of His mercy. He saved us through the washing of rebirth and renewal by the Holy Spirit, whom He poured out on us generously through Jesus Christ our Savior, so that, having been justified by His grace, we might become heirs having the hope of eternal life (Titus 3:5–7).

God desires for us to experience more than a "taste" of His goodness. He desires us to live and grow through a lifelong journey.

Jesus provided the Holy Spirit's miraculous infilling to equip believers for healing, power-endued ministry, and victorious living. I was ignorant of the fullness of God's Holy Spirit. No one ever taught me. Therefore, I did not understand how the Spirit could live within me. Little did I know at first that, as the new birth brings us into eternal life and prepares us for heaven, so the fullness of the Spirit equips our present life with authority, power, healing, joy, and peace. A piece of heaven deposited into our being:

In order that we, who were the first to hope in Christ, might be for the praise of his glory. And you also were included in Christ when you heard the word of truth, the gospel of your salvation. Having believed, you were marked in him with a seal, the promised Holy Spirit, who is a deposit guaranteeing our inheritance until the redemption of those who are God's possession—to the praise of his glory.

Ephesians 1:12–14

For a season, I was like an eager puppy following my "Ananias" around and draining the wisdom out of her. Vicki D. told me that I did not drain her. She told me I gave her as much as she gave me. She even told me God had placed me in her heart and praised Him because if not, I surely would have run her off. So often, in our healing, we unknowingly help others as well as ourselves. As long as we are stepping up, we are useful for God's Kingdom.

For two years straight, I read Scripture endlessly. It nourished me! The New Testament is covenant guaranteed, and I suddenly understood that the Old Testament was pointing me to the cross, a beautiful tapestry of prophecy and symbolism. The Comforter or Holy Spirit remains available to the church until Jesus' return (1 Corinthians 1:7). The spiritual gifts have not ceased. The Spirit is the seal on the promise of healing that is inherent to His covenant people. Not everyone experiences these things exactly as I did. God ordains a spiritual journey custom-suited to each saint. The fullness of Christ in us, however, is available to everyone who receives Him.

Sometimes, the infilling of the Holy Spirit accompanies our salvation. Sometimes, it comes later, as it did for me. Before I received the infilling, I definitely felt the Holy Spirit move in my life. But I had not yet come to a place where I had a limitless source, an overflowing well of God's love. I kept too many obstacles in place.

Upon receiving salvation, we have access to the indwelling of the Spirit. The Spirit's intent is to reside in us full-time and overflow out of us. This is the completeness that requires us to surrender our desires and seek only Him. We do this by faith and with a willingness to receive what He offers.

Among the gifts of the Spirit are the word of wisdom and the word of knowledge. I have experienced both. These gifts and others are listed in 1 Corinthians 12:7–11. I also have a prayer language; Romans 8:26–27 supports this truth.

The gifts empower us to minister to others. Over the years, I have witnessed physical and emotional healings by God through His saints. Since that day in Vicki D.'s office, I received discernment and a teaching gift that surpasses my capabilities (Ephesians 4:11). I just believe God's entire Word, and I remain open to His work in me and through me.

As I suggested earlier, the infilling of the Holy Spirit can occur twenty years after salvation is received. The promise of the Spirit relies on our surrender and God's order, which is specific to the need. Three specific examples in the Book of Acts teach us not to presume that everyone must follow the same order: they are Acts 2:38, 8:15, and 10:47.

God poured out His Spirit in all three cases. The truth that is fundamental to all three is this: we need the fullness of His Spirit to walk in freedom during our lives. This seal is a deposit, earnest, or a piece or promise of heaven on earth (Ephesians 1:14). As Matthew 6:10 (NIV) tells us, "On earth as it is in heaven!" I ask God every day for a fresh infilling and ask the Holy Spirit to please comfort me and remove my fear.

I believe there is a healing for you; it is found in the pages of the Bible, in the power of the resurrection, and through the infilling to the fullness of the Holy Spirit that can accompany you through life. I thought I understood this when I accepted Christ as a teen, but I was missing the power that was available. I also blocked that power with my choices and I continue to block it when I decide to revert back to old methods/strongholds/sins that are not His intention for my life; remember, this is a life-long journey. My salvation was a mixture of the right words and the wrong actions, including severe disobedience on my part. I was all talk and very little walk.

Sadly, if we are not vigilant, salvation can quickly become an event that happened in the past. When the Bible is just a story to us, when we pick and choose the parts to which we will adhere, we end up sitting atop a dunghill of denial. On that heap of hopelessness, we often inadvertently deny the deliverance of healing that we desperately need.

While the Spirit enters the believer upon salvation, few people release enough faith to allow the fullness or infilling of the Spirit to reside within them. Too often, our Sunday schools get stuck in the comfortable zone of teaching about Noah's Ark, the whale's belly, and the manger. Few venture far enough to get the children filled up with the fullness of the Holy Spirit. I believe this is the very reason our society is hurting; we are missing this critical step. Therefore, we lack the capacity to understand His ways and bring healing. Without His Counselor, the Holy Spirit, we can do neither.

We need to be filled to overflowing. Raise your hands! Yes, right, now set the book down and raise your hands. Praise Him. Sing to Him. Love Him. Drink Him into your hurting heart. Then lie down with your face in the floor and tell Him you are sorry. Tell Him you want His blood covering, the fullness of His infilling, and His healing. Believe, have faith, and let your emotions play catch-up later. Many times, faith involves believing the truth of God's promises even before we see their truth in our lives.

If you desire to be filled in this way, pray this prayer:

I believe in Jesus Christ. He is God's son. He died for my sins. He was resurrected. After He arose, I believe God deployed His Holy Spirit so the promise of His life could live inside of me. Seal me, Father. I no longer wish to tap into the power of Your Holy Spirit. I want You to unpack the power inside my being and take up residence. Forgive me, Jesus! I choose to have my flesh die for You, Christ. Replace all of me with You. Baptize me in your Holy Spirit in Jesus' name.

Allow your faith to meet His faithfulness. If you are still struggling with this death to self and the infilling of His Spirit, do not give up. "God things" rarely happen according to our plans. Feeling unsure or fearful is normal. This will make more sense as you gain more knowledge. We still have twelve chapters to go, and I promise to do my part. I know God always does His.

We are walking the steps of healing from death into life—my death into life and your death into life. As you read, you may remember having already experienced this transformation in some area of your life. You may be rejoicing and praising God at this very moment. You may also be in desperate need of healing in some other areas. I pray now that you will surrender the pain and allow your feet to step up, up, up, and into the Holy of Holies where Jesus lives within us—"Christ in you the hope of glory" (Colossians 1:27, NIV).

The experience brings me back to the song "Masquerade" that I referenced in the Introduction. The lyrics describe what was going on in my heart when I began to catch those glimmers of promise.

Hope was beginning to rise up inside me. It didn't happen all at once. You might still feel hopeless. That is okay; you are in the process of healing. If this stepping upward were easy, you would have done it years ago. He can restore and replace what you feel you have lost. As He said in Joel 2:25 (KJV), "I will restore to you the years that the locust hath eaten…"

One day, my son came running into the bathroom, gasping for air, and said, "Mom, there is a locust outside. He is blackish-green with wings and bulging eyes. What does he eat? Will he bite me?"

I could not help but reply, "No, sweetheart. If he is in our yard, he is very full from eating all of Mommy's years." I figured I would explain the conundrum later.

The point is that healing becomes obvious over time. The more your divine purpose peeks above the surface, the easier it is to make your way up the staircase. Inch by inch, you begin to realize that you have the faith you need to be healed and stay healed.

The more we see God's changes within us and believe His Word as truth, the stronger our faith becomes. Increasingly, faith strengthens hope, as Hebrews 11:1 (KJV) reveals, "Now faith is the substance of things hoped for, the evidence of things not seen." This is when healing becomes real to us.

The Spirit does the work, and we realize God is transforming us, not through our physical strength or ability, but by His Spirit. We begin to notice that being sober, healthy, or peaceful is easier with the passing of each successful day. Before this point, faith is similar to hope; both involve a belief in what is unseen. When healing occurs, faith becomes the substance or tangible truth of what Scripture promises.

Well done! Remove the mask of denial and continue to check and see if it has tried to resurface. I have had to pry it off my face a hundred times!

CHAPTER TWO

WE ARE NOT THE ULTIMATE AUTHORITY

STEP TWO: RELINQUISH CONTROL, BY FAITH

"And I will put My Spirit in you and move you to follow My decrees and be careful to keep my laws"

(Ezekiel 36:27, NIV)

Trying to control your world is as helpful as attempting to exit the room of your pain by stepping out of a window: If the window is high enough, control is exactly what you lose. If the window is low enough, you could end up under the control of a briar bush.

We need to realize that when we think we are in control of things or people, we are actually making self-sabotaging and even life-threatening decisions. Control has no upside. God intended us to permit only His control in our lives. His control is real power. When combined with our faith, it is the force that brings healing. On this step, we should at least be allowing Scripture to enter our ear gate, whether by the incorporation that has been diligently placed in the prior chapters, by hearing a sermon, or by reading for ourselves.

In fact, the window in the maskquerade was inoperable, hidden, and too small to get through. Any windows that are part of our pain will always be too small to serve as exits. We stand at these openings and holler for help. In reality, the deadbolt has already been unlocked with the key of our salvation in Christ. Yet, there we remain stuck screaming in satan's employment pool.

We refuse to do the very thing that would free us. We refuse to release control and let God help us turn the doorknob. As long as we refuse, the unturned knob prevents us from leaving.

There are as many ways to stay in control as there are people. A few methods I used were justification, pride, depression, blame, judgment, false opinions, and a victim mentality. To these seven, I added a twist of manipulation and stubbornness. The sad part was my failure to realize that I was operating deceitfully. We rarely see our sin.

My irrational need to control people, emotions, circumstances, and surroundings was rooted in deeper issues like fear covered in anger. The demand I had on myself to stay in a very broken marriage. It was keeping me sick. What I thought was holding everything together was the very thing tearing me apart. The devil is an expert at keeping us tied up in the incidentals so that we overlook the real issues and the bigger picture of our purpose.

Eventually, I recognized that I was the one keeping me sick. I stepped out of the denial, but I was still so overwhelmed in sickness that the root cause seemed impossible to fix. This is the place where we so often give up because, until we accept the fact that we are incapable of fixing ourselves, we will not release the pain to God.

Which methods do you see yourself using to control your pain? Do you employ any of the methods I mentioned? Look deep into your heart and allow God to reveal any devices you are using. And know this: At some point, we all depend on something to stay in control. If that something is not God, then the hurt will resurface.

The Blame Game

I was convinced my pain was justified. There was always a good reason: the way my parents raised me, my first husband's behavior, or the weather that day. I could not assume blame. My pride had to stay intact. The shell of arrogance was the only thing holding me up. So, often, we find an overinflated ego attached to severe pain. I see anger and pride as the reverse of depression, even as far as to say it is our evil nature attempting to create depression in others, yet we use both to hide and control our hurt.

When we point fingers, we operate in a false sense of control. We think that blaming someone or something else frees us from responsibility for our actions. We even think hurting others will somehow relieve our pain. Never the case! Therefore, we believe we are still in control. The only thing we are still controlling is the duration of our pain. We keep the pain from healing and ensure a longer battle! In our ignorance, we think we have found a scapegoat who will accept the guilty verdict for us. It is one of satan's favorite methods for keeping us in bondage.

Opinions that do not line up directly with Scripture keep us bound. The certainty of God's Word is where we must base our claims. That is where we can experience freedom. We also need to realize that the people in our lives have no control over our healing. As long as we listen to God, He can heal us—even if their behavior defies our standards and His.

God has our best interests at heart. We are responsible for choosing His ways over ours and the devil's. The devil wants us to think letting go is scary, but it is not scary to let God heal you. Either way, 2 Timothy 1:7 says, "God has not given us a spirit of fear, but of power and of love and of a sound mind."

Accepting Jesus was the beginning of my healing. Inviting the fullness of His Holy Spirit activated the actual manifestation of healing in my life. This is the subject many churches and Bible studies do not cover. The infilling is where true healing and power reside.

It comes down to being willing to let go completely. We need to be totally emancipated from our control if we are to obtain God's healing, gifts, and power. We cannot expect to remain in ultimate authority over our lives and be healed.

Same Ole, Same Ole

It was the same old routine. I had been there before. I knelt and then fell to the floor in tears. With my head on my hands, I rolled myself up into as tight a ball as I could. All I wanted was to protect myself from any more abuse and pain. The problem is that, for the most part, the worst pain wasn't all the broken and smashed items or the cuts and bruises; it was what I was, that sinking feeling on the inside.

Unable to withstand any more hurt, I ached and felt like life had ripped my heart out of my chest. My tears fell. Hyperventilation hindered my breathing. My body was in the fetal position that innately I knew I needed to take as a representation of a new birth, but every time, uncurling to go back to the dog's vomit instead of my Father's love. I found myself in this position too often when my first husband was around.

"Why me?" I asked. Another syndrome is the all too popular "why me" syndrome. "Why do I have to endure this awful pain and abuse? Why do I have to feel paralyzed by fear every day? What can I blame? Whose fault can it be? If I blame him, then I must leave. How can I keep the bad feelings from surfacing again?"

I sincerely wanted answers to these questions, all while choosing to stay in a marriage that was not meant to be, and that is an understatement. I think we all do this at times, especially when we are either unaware of how to stop the pain the easy way or confused as to how to get rid of it—for good because we are excusing flat-out abuse because we are scared to walk away.

Instead of remaining prostrate before God, knowing I was surrendering to the pain by staying and that He had the rest under control, I would eventually get off the floor, stand up, and answer my own questions. Then, I would find an excuse or a worldly method to sweep the pain under the rug and keep it there for as long as I could. I was scared. It was a vicious cycle that stole almost two decades of my life. Do not let your fear of the unknown steal any more years from you. He loves you, and your healing is His top priority.

I would remove the mask of oppression to the abuse (or so I thought) by embracing the mask of pride and arrogance. It wasn't enough. However, even at the height of my control, I still felt exposed, as though everyone knew about my pain despite my mask. I still felt vulnerable, weak, incapable, and sick.

Our improper, calculating attempts to fix/comfort things over which we have no power keep us powerless. Ironic, isn't it? Satan and our need for control have us trapped in the maskquerade, hurting behind a closed (yet unlocked, unlatched) door. Although denial is gone, we still find it hard to release our hold. It is tough to let go, and it is a process. Isn't it odd that when denial abates, leaving us glaring straight into the face of our issue, we still choose comfort over ablation?

We have claimed ownership, yet we are shocked and rightfully intimidated by the issue. The fear of our lack drives us to "manage" our feelings of inadequacy by quitting. In fear, we attempt to shift even deeper into control. Instead of steadily moving upward, we step off to the side and withdraw from the fight. Why? Because now the battle is real, and we need help stepping out and up.

What we fail to realize is that we will always lack something, but God is sufficient. With Him, we need never give up. He created us. He knows how to care for our every need.

The only thing we accomplish by giving up is to create a mudslide next to our step. It is a bad place to be. The footing is treacherous, and we can slip back into denial if we are not careful.

When the desire to quit in fear rises up inside, we need to stay alert. Instead of choosing to control the situation, we must choose to trust God to heal us. We need to opt out of taking control. The truth is we have no control, but God does.

Do you believe God can handle all the details of your healing? Are you willing to trade your control for His power? Do you understand only your free will can keep the door to freedom closed?

Orange Bottles of Pseudo Peace

I reached into the tiny opening in the pill bottle and pinched a pill between my first two fingers. I could do it in the dark, and most times, I did. My fingers went too far into the bottle. That meant my supply was dwindling. When pill shortages occurred (and they were often), I immediately felt panic sweep over me. My chest tightened, my stomach soured, and a breathless, threatening fear set in.

I struggled to pull in some air, knowing I would now have to manipulate somebody in order to get a refill. The insurance company monitored the timing of my refills, but I did not care. I would pay out of pocket if necessary. The doctor stood between me and my supply; I would have to get her to agree with me, even though the insurance and pharmaceutical laws backed her up.

The obstacles were plentiful. All I wanted was to be in control. Control would quiet the panic. I would feel safe, if only for a time. Control is deceptive. It provides a sense of healing that is nothing more than a counterfeit.

It was all to escape something much deeper: a loss of foundation as a child, a demand to have a "foundation" as an adult for me and my children, even if the "foundation" was rotten. Fear kept me bound to my circumstances, and so I ran with fervor to everything wrong, anything to try and escape my responsibility to step out and up!

Acknowledging the devious and debilitating nature of denial and control will help open the door to healing. Be aware, however, that denial and control will try to weave themselves into every issue that comes up. We need wisdom to recognize and eradicate bad habits that attempt to surface or resurface. We must be aware that satan whispers in our ears. We must be quick to shut him down.

I did not know what to do with the symptoms plaguing me and the passion for someone to love and respect me. My "solution" (a wrong, unhelpful approach) was to numb myself with substances and guard the mess with pride. It was my feeble attempt to control my out-of-control situation. These attempts were exhausting. Manipulation always causes more damage, more pain, and more issues.

Do you see similar tendencies in your life? Can you identify areas that you attempt to control? Are they typically related to your emotions, physical appearance, surroundings, circumstances, or other people? When the devil comes calling, are you willing to resist him? Here is a tip: Scripture tells us an order, and there is a step before "resisting the devil." It is "submit" to God.

Afraid to Be Free

There are so many memories from the years of my captivity—the hiding... feelings of inadequacy...fear of weakness...the destructive behaviors designed to camouflage my overwhelming insecurities.

There was never a shortage of control devices in my arsenal. Smoking was one. I remember how my nervous hand shook as I inhaled the smoke into my lungs. My fear of being seen smoking made me nervous. When sober, I could never have a cigarette without feeling guilty.

Like any other vice, there is always the issue of supply. Just like the pills, my cigarettes kept running out. I remember buying them more than I remember smoking them. The same was true for the beer I bought at the convenience store. The smell of gasoline and the shade of the gas port became as familiar as home to me.

This was the life I was used to living. It had become a kind of comfort zone—so much that when I arrived at the door of freedom and noticed that the deadbolt was disengaged, I wanted to reengage the lock. I would not relinquish control of my habits. I refused to allow God to open the door. I was afraid of all the pain that would manifest the minute I became sober. I was not trusting God to be my comfort.

Do you believe that God can comfort you and protect you as He heals you?

It sounds hard to believe, but we are often more afraid of healing than we are of being sick. We see the sickness as a safe place, an evil cushion of familiarity, if only because the unknown is intimidating. Please let me give you hope: Familiarity is not the answer. We have a far better solution in God. His Holy Spirit fills and heals us. It is the closest thing to heaven on this earth. There is no reason to give up. Healing need not frighten us!

In this world, God's truths are often disregarded or forgotten; that is the reason sickness is so prevalent. If you have not received the fullness of His

Spirit, ask Him. Keep asking Him until you get it. The Gospel of Luke assures us of His desire to fill us: "If you then, though you are evil, know how to give good gifts to your children, how much more will your Father in Heaven give the Holy Spirit to those who ask him!" (Luke 11:13, NIV)

Remember, He does not expect us to be certain about those first steps. I wasn't. I proceeded with trepidation and uncertainty, not really wanting to move. We are not supposed to be certain. This is the step where faith comes in and fills the gap.

Freedom from Alcohol and Nicotine

The garage in our second home is a room I will never forget. God got my attention there. It was several years into my first marriage, but before I discovered God's fullness, I was in the worst stage of my alcohol and nicotine addictions and, of course, a bad place in the marriage.

One evening, during my late twenties, I stood in that garage, inebriated and listening to the radio. I had already told God, a bazillion times, that I had taken my last dance with the devil. I kept promising to get sober. This time was different: I admitted my inability to get sober and asked Him to do it.

The only station I could get in that garage was a Christian radio station. A praise song came on, and I began to dance, this time with God. I praised Him and thanked Him for the life I did feel in those moments when I allowed it. I cried with my hands raised and thanked Him for my children and Jesus. I danced, wept, laughed, and believed with faith for my Savior.

Worship comes before warfare. Ground was about to be taken. I did not know at the time that Jesus had already gone to hell and paid for this exact sliver of my life. I did not realize He had already done the work for me, but He had.

In our weakness, He is strong. I screamed out the name that is above all names: "Jesus! Jesus! Jesus! Heal me. Save me. Make me okay with You. Help me to understand You. I release the control of alcohol and cigarettes on my life."

On that night, I gave that part of my heart to Him. Loving Father that He is, He gave it back to me healed. I was free from the addiction to alcohol and cigarettes in an instant! Like a child, I sought God's face. I worshiped Him at one of the lowest points in my life. He knew I was steeped in brokenness, wallowing in the pit of addiction, control, anxiety, and fear. It was then that He turned the tide.

Notice that I spoke aloud to the exact hurt that needed healing. Speak to your disease, issue, or pain directly. Command it to leave in Jesus' name and by the power of Christ's blood.

Now, I was ready to let go of the alcohol and cigarettes. He took them; I was healed from the very thing I was ready to give Him. All we have to do is be ready to let go of the issue and then release it fully. Whatever piece we hold on to in an effort to control the situation will keep us sick.

How many times had I cried out to Him before this eventful night? I cannot say. But all of my pleas cumulated in this very precious moment. Somehow, my wrong way of dealing had shifted; I moved out of control mode and into humility. I allowed my hunger for help and healing to be seen. I trusted His ability to provide for me. I believed that He was enough for me and able to replace the habit with wholeness.

My trust in Him and my release of control were all that were necessary for God to deliver me in that moment. It was a beautiful step into faith. God was real, and so was His healing. We were building a bond of trust together. Several years later, I allowed Him deeper access to soften my heart, which gradually gave Him access to more of my broken heart and soul.

I did not realize at that moment, still in my late twenties, that my garage deliverance was a miracle. I still had stuff in my pocket that I was not ready to give up. Until I decided to give it all up in my thirties, I was keeping myself hindered from seeing the fullness of what had occurred. I entered the right process but continued to hold out on God. I allowed a partial work, which we all so often do, but He promises us in Philippians 1:6 that if we allow Him, He will finish the good work.

Step Forward by His Spirit

Each time we take a step forward, He is pleased. His yoke is easy and His burden is light (Matthew 11:30). Often, we say, "I could never please God, so why even try?" That is another form of control. Giving up and perfectionism—the all-or-nothing approaches to life—are control issues. They have no place in the Kingdom. Giving up or trying too hard with the arm of the flesh is why we are sick to begin with. Jesus is the only example of perfection; the rest of us fall short (Romans 3:23).

Now, we are not to disregard the command of Matthew 5:48 (NIV): "Be perfect, therefore, as your heavenly Father is perfect." There is a difference between perfectionism and the godly striving toward Christ's likeness. The latter is about allowing the Holy Spirit to sanctify us. The former is about us trying to paint the perfect picture of self.

Zechariah 4:6 (NIV) warns, "'Not by might nor by power, but by My Spirit,' says the LORD Almighty." I will remind you of this verse often. We must accept our imperfections as we navigate up the stairs. Healing happens when we release control for refinement into His image, knowing that we are incapable of succeeding without His Spirit.

In that garage, God and I had a moment of healing and trust that superseded anything I had ever known. He gave me a taste of freedom, and I held that flavor in the understanding of my heart. This step defined my faith for the next level of healing level. In the exuberance that freedom brings, we can still make excuses for dilly-dallying on a certain step.

I was not ready to die out yet and still quite blind. What an example of trying to be in command of our destiny. There is always this resistance to allowing God to rule it all. You can see how many wrong methods I used to attempt to break free and how hesitant I was to release total control. I had a crowbar wedged in the door that led to freedom, but I also had my head hanging out the window, hollering, "Victim!" On both sides of the issue, I tried to exert my control over God's.

Looking back, my sin seems so obvious, sad, and strange, but in the midst of the battle, I was either oblivious or scared of my failure to please God. Now that alcohol and cigarettes were abandoned, I attached my foolish affections more strongly to the orange opaque bottles full of temporary peace and the crumbling marriage I was so afraid to let go of.

Finally, I had left the denial and control around my alcoholism and smoking at the foot of the cross. Those sins had been visible to all—and they were ugly. The ones I still had were more subtle and easier to hide. Therefore, I kept them and the mindset of sickness and death that accompanied them.

First Timothy 5:24 (NIV) explains, "The sins of some men are obvious, reaching the place of judgment ahead of them; the sins of others trail behind them."

My knee-jerk response to confusion and pain was to foolishly assume that I had control of my environment. I was confused as to what happened with the alcohol, and I was scared to accept it as a miracle from God. If it had been a miracle, then I would have to trust God with my other issues. So, I decided to cope with my remaining "stuff" by managing my surroundings. Instead of getting better, I decided to buy a better house. We were not yet trusting the truth that...His power is sufficient.

Too often, we purchase boats, cars, planes, houses, clothes, vacations, club memberships, and countless other things as a way to fill the void only God's fullness can satisfy. Now, I know we need some of these things, but we are all aware there is also a stuff syndrome. When we buy to supply satisfaction, we are attempting to control our pain by altering our surroundings. Ignorance works temporarily, at least until our nagging pain reveals that the only thing we changed was the wallpaper.

My first husband and I purchased our third home just as I was sobering up, by God's grace, from my fourteen-year bout with beer, wine, and cigarettes. However, I was knee-deep in the medicine chest and neck-deep in my own power. It was like being in the purgatory room at The Masquerade; I wasn't in hell yet and a long way from heaven. I did make an unwanted visit down there, and I will share it with you along the way; I stumbled in the pit from direct disobedience to God. Fear and reverence I now own in generous proportion.

When we are mired in transition, we need to keep forging ahead, remembering His good work scripture, "Being confident of this, that He who began a good work in you will carry it on to completion until the day of Christ Jesus" (Philippians 1:6, NIV). Only He can bring us out of life's purgatories and into heaven on earth.

As I tried to fill the void left by the departure of alcohol and cigarettes from my daily routine, I made sure my bag contained a variety of colored pills and my credit card. Drugs, shopping, and a bigger house were suddenly my addictions of choice. But even the house did not hold up. Like me and my first marriage, it was sinking. Our home seemed as broken and messed up as our hearts and minds.

Matthew described the condition well:

The rain came down, the streams rose, and the winds blew and beat against that house; yet it did not fall because it had its foundation on the rock. But everyone who hears these words of mine and does not put them into practice is like a foolish man who built his house on sand. The rain came down, the streams rose, and the winds blew and beat against that house, and it fell with a great crash.

Matthew 7:25–27 (NIV)

Our new home was not built on a solid rock. Over the period of mere months, the front of the house separated from the front porch. New cracks were forming before our eyes. Our kitchen ceiling rippled like waves of sand on a beach. Every corner of the house had separated. The brick was cracked all over.

When I bathed, I looked up at an actual cardboard box top covering a hole in our ceiling and prayed no rain would drive it into the tub with me. We had to remove walls and portions of the roof and cover them in plastic. When I got out of bed, the cold from the concrete floor shot up through my legs. I almost longed for the warm, soft carpet that had been in place before the toxic mold infestation required its removal.

The shower in the master bath sank downward along with the foundation. It was unusable for almost two years. Both the kitchen ceiling and the driveway parted like the Red Sea. Tiles cracked, and the mortar fell away. The huge front palladium window shattered and stayed that way for several years. Like my attempts at control, the inoperable window served as a weak substitute for genuine protection. I stood vulnerable behind that window, both literally and figuratively.

Many times, you have to look hard at the outside of a structure to detect damage; ours was not one of those cases. The calamity was self-evident. On a spiritual level, the life of denying our idolatry and the effort to control sin without God's power did not create pictures of calamity as profound as the sight of our dying house. Nevertheless, what happens behind the scenes eventually shows up on some level. We will sink if we do not allow God to ground us in the Word and build us upon the solid rock.

We must constantly take heed and step carefully. Moving forward without God is costly. Missteps always lead downward—down and back into control and denial. We need to release control of our emotions and environment; we need to trust God. When we head in His direction, focus on our responsibilities, and stop blaming others, we heal. God then restores, rebuilds, and renews:

> *Give us gladness in proportion to our former misery! Replace the evil years with good. Let us, Your servants, see You work again; let our children see Your glory. And may the Lord our God show us His approval and make our efforts successful. Yes, make our efforts successful!*

> Psalm 90:15–17 (NLT)

Faith Is the Action Piece

Our awareness for stepping out of control is faith. We will have faith to believe that God is in control and will take care of us so we can remove the mask of denial and control. We will base our lives on the faith that we have obtained by His Word as truth for our lives, described by Hebrews 11:6.

And without faith, it is impossible to please God because anyone who comes to Him must believe that He exists and that He rewards those who earnestly seek Him.

Trust is not an all-or-nothing virtue. It is one that grows and develops the deeper we go into relationship with God. As we step up in His Word, so does our faith.

Your transitions are individual, yet they share certain characteristics with those that occur in the lives of believers across the globe. The bottom line is to accept and serve Christ in everything. If the window keeps us half in and half out of the fullness He offers, why not trust God to see us all the way through in all the right ways? When we leave the need for control behind us for good, we can move on to the next step of the journey.

For now, let me say that I am so proud of your perseverance! You are moving up and being healed. Be patient; do not give up. With your newfound faith, God can now answer your prayers. Believe me, He is faithful!

If you still feel unsure about the things we are discussing, you are normal. Let me share a secret: just love God with all your heart and trust that He will work in your life. It is okay to wonder about what has happened in your life so far and to be a bit timid of your future if you are hurting. As you release your sin and pain to Him, it will all begin to make sense.

Be willing to step up; also, be willing to retrace the previous step if you need to. Whatever you do, please do not stop! Keep releasing yourself into His hands and trust Him. You are healing!

Congratulations! You have stepped out of control. You have also added the awareness of faith and know of the baptism of the Holy Spirit (Acts 1:5). God sees your hard work. He is proud of you, and so am I. You are beautiful and getting stronger every day!

Step up, mighty mask remover, step up!

Chapter Three

SUBMIT TO THE KING AND BE HEALED

Step Three: Surrender to God in Prayer

"But He gives us more grace. That is why Scripture says, 'God opposes the proud but gives grace to the humble." Submit yourselves, then, to God. Resist the devil, and he will flee from you'

(James 4:6–7, NIV)

God intended for us to be friends with Him. So often, we revere Him to the extent that we are willing to prepare an Easter basket or place a manger on the mantel. As we blaze through life in our fury and all on our pagan calendar. When Christmas ends, we take Him down, the same way we do the pilgrim doll when Thanksgiving is over. On December 26, we store the manger in the attic for another year.

This is not God's desire for our relationship with Him. He wants us to take Him off the mantel and allow Him to be our mantle every day. In order to be healed and stay healed, we must deepen our intimacy with Him.

When we do this, our friendship with God comes to life. The free-will door on our maskquerade is always ready to open if we are willing. We are free to welcome His ways and gain access to the narrow stairway leading to the holiest place on earth, The Holy of Holies, God's presence. If you get into an intimate place with God, which takes surrender, He will heal you.

It hinders our healing to pretend that God cannot be our friend. We revere Him, of course. But is our version of reverence pleasing to Him or to us? The issue is whether or not we have cultivated an intimate daily relationship with Him. Why is it so hard to believe that He wants to know us personally? Why do we attempt to regulate our relationship with God according to secular or "religious" expectations and rules?

God is the great I Am. He is perfect, and He is perfect love. Many of us have been hurt, abandoned, rejected, smothered, or controlled by our earthly parental figures. As a result, we project their characteristics onto God. It is a fallacious view because God's love is flawless. If a family member inflicted pain, your intimacy with your Heavenly Father is the only cure for the sting.

As I was healing and being filled with the fullness of God's Holy Spirit, I could not understand why I felt so bothered by the way my parents raised me. I honor them and love them for the provision and love they provided. However, I had to work through my pain for years and still do on some level. If we think we can quit, we are fooling ourselves. I needed God to restore the lack of spiritual truth presented in our home (even though, from a worldly perspective, the deficiency looked normal).

My frustration made sense when I found three key scriptures:

"Fathers, do not exasperate your children; instead, bring them up in the training and instruction of the Lord" (Ephesians 6:4, NIV).

"Whoever spares the rod hates their children, but the one who loves their children is careful to discipline them" (Proverbs 13:24, NIV).

"Train a child up in the way he should go and when he is old he will not turn from it" (Proverbs 22:6; see also Deuteronomy 6:7; Proverbs 14:26 and 22:15, NASB).

Feeling cheated and upset because your parents did not raise you in the knowledge of God is scriptural. However, we must not hold resentment in our hearts or sin in our anger. We must forgive and move past our irritation, knowing that God can make of our pain a blessing to help others who have struggled with the same issues. Many people need to know they are not alone. In order to heal, they need to understand their feelings of frustration are shared. Your journey up the stairs is for you and for others.

Whatever our spiritual heritage (even if there seems to be none), we tend to perpetuate the religious design our family established for us. We then attempt to relate to God according to their rules and expectations. But what if their ways are not pleasing to God? Often in Scripture, we see that God desires a remnant who will return to His ways and establish a line that pleases Him. We need to continually evaluate our beliefs and allow God to deconstruct and reconstruct them as He sees fit.

Our lack of godly guidance can restrict our ability to go deep with God. I even have friends who grew up with weekly doses of "religion," but their problem was their "religion" was missing a relationship with God's heart. On this third step, we will learn how to surrender our preconceived notions through prayer. We will then discover the freedom to receive the godly guidance we once lacked.

First, let me say this: God is my best friend ever. Let Him be yours. Put on no pretense, render no judgment, and subject His love to no human ideals. Do not allow anyone else to define God for you. Embrace Him by reading both Testaments, by praying, and by walking with Him in friendship daily:

Take to heart Paul's admonition about the "religious" people of his day:

Since they did not know the righteousness that comes from God and sought to establish their own, they did not submit to God's righteousness. Christ is the end of the law so that there may be righteousness for everyone who believes.

Romans 10:3–4 (NIV)

The White Flag of Surrender

Surrender shows humility. It reveals your willingness to be exposed to God. Humility will cause you to open the door you thought protected you. God tells us that humility comes from wisdom. Letting go of control, the power to influence or direct behavior or events in the last chapter, and giving us the gift of faith sounds oddly familiar to surrender. However, surrender is defined more as submitting to authority, hence the scripture reference at the start of this chapter.

We need to first let go of thinking we have power. Then, we can capitulate to God's love with godly sorrow, opening our hands and releasing our grip on our lives. We can then place our palms on the door of self-protection and push through. Surrendering to Christ and to the fullness of God's Holy Spirit will lead us into an intimate relationship with Him. This is where healing is accessible.

Once we release our grip on our lives, we can surrender our lives to Christ. That means releasing everything to Him. This humility will bring the realization that we need to yield to Him daily, if not hourly.

Paul described the yielding this way: "I face death every day—yes, just as surely as I boast about you in Christ Jesus our Lord" (1 Corinthians 15:31, NIV).

If freedom is what we desire, we will surrender our ownership of the whole lot. We will give in to God's authority, and we will let Him fight for us.

This walk is one of continually submitting and resubmitting to Christ. We may feel that we have already done so or at least done so in a particular area, yet we may need to surrender again. When pain persists, we must find the area in which we have not yet chosen Him over the pain.

The time to choose Him is today—every day. There is always another opportunity to surrender to Him again. Make it a daily habit, just as Paul did.

As long as we surrender, He will guide us up the steps at His speed. We might wish we had surrendered earlier, but He is patient and forgiving with us. We need to be open to Him on this step. From our salvation experience, we know what surrender feels like. Now, we need to get used to living in a surrendered state. We can do this through prayer; therefore, we will birth a healthy prayer life on this step.

God should be your best friend. He has an intimate plan for you; that plan is bound by love. All Kingdom relationships are based on love, as Colossians 3:14 (NIV) reveals: "And over all these virtues put on love, which binds them all together in perfect unity."

Walk hand in hand with Christ and share every trial with Him. Do you long for His company? In what ways have you surrendered to Him? Are you still unsure? Ask Him to comfort you and help you. He will teach you how to let Him in so that you can be healed.

More Walk, Less Talk

As we begin to implement our awareness, it is important to understand the power behind each act. The power of removing the masks of denial, control, and fear into true surrender to be what God intended. We need to have our hearts open, and that is a vulnerable place for many people. These foundational biblical techniques are designed to build gradually, one upon the other, to gently ensure healing.

You have already accomplished two actions, adding hope and faith, each connected with their respective steps. Now, take them with you on each subsequent step, along with the third action showing your awareness, which is prayer.

Awareness is employed throughout your lifetime: hope, faith, prayer, reading, worship, rest, fasting, listening, giving, serving, studying His Word, functioning in your purpose, and functioning in His love.

During this surrender step, I will stress the importance of a consistent prayer life. Prayer will help us to remain faithful to the remaining actions. The life of faith is one of knowing and doing. We have to walk the talk. As James wrote, "Don't just listen to God's word. You must do what it says. Otherwise, you are only fooling yourselves" (James 1:22, NLT). Do what it says! James does not tell us what to believe in. He tells us what to do because of what we believe in.

Part of walking the talk is surrendering ourselves daily in prayer, asking for His will to be done (Matthew 6:10). We need to understand that prayer deals with situations in the spiritual realms first. Our trials are of a spiritual nature and begin in the heavenlies. Paul taught as much: For our struggle is not against flesh and blood, but against the rulers, against the authorities, against the powers of this dark world, and against the spiritual forces of evil in the heavenly realms (Ephesians 6:12, NIV).

The heavenly realms is where satan, the accuser of the brethren, resides (Zechariah. 3:1–2; Job 1:6–12). When we pray, spiritual warfare is activated in the heavenlies first. Then, as God releases His angels, power, and truth, the healing (reconciliation, resolution, restoration) filters down into the natural realm. His order, which is opposite to what our flesh desires, is thereby reestablished.

We begin our prayers by requesting His forgiveness for our sins and then asking Him to reveal the things we do not see. He needs to reveal the hidden areas that have arisen from our sickness, the areas that are not pleasing to Him. The attitude we need to assume is reflected in Psalm 139:23–24 (NLT): "Search me, O God, and know my heart; test me and know my anxious thoughts. See if there is any offensive way in me, and lead me in the way everlasting."

The binding mechanism in our prayer is faith. Our last awareness gave us exactly what we need to reach God. Faith is inside you. The disciples did not ask Jesus to teach them to preach; they asked Him to teach them to pray. If all you can do is recite the Lord's Prayer from Matthew 6:9–13, then do that. If not, just talk with the Lord and ask Him to teach you to pray.

When you arrive at this step, you have admitted your need for healing and our responsibility to seek it. The door to your heart and soul is open and ready for God to work. After mastering the first two steps, you should feel a release of some of the pressure you were under. It may be only a small improvement, but take note of it. Do not allow the devil to subvert your healing by diminishing it. You are progressing. With God, the progression is real, and the healing is gradual because He is working to heal you from the inside out. It takes time.

We move upward by asking forgiveness and submitting to God's order through prayer. Here, we begin to establish useful, healthy habits for a fruitful life. We are submitted only to the battles God would have us fight, a cease-fire for the devil. (Have you raised a white flag in any areas of your life yet?)

Vulnerability is not comfortable, but it is a good place to be. There, we can cut loose of all the junk that has hardened our hearts, fragmented our souls, and caused bad roots to take hold. The hand of God holds us up and cleans us out. We must relax, rest, and allow Him to work in our lives.

God will take us up and through each step. Challenging emotions may surface; we may not even understand them all. But they will subside. Be prayerful not to allow the emotion to rule. Choose to be still. God will shape and change us in this molding stage. As far as God is concerned, where there is willingness, there is a way.

We must be vulnerable and open to God. That is part of walking the talk.

The Saint and the Sinner

After more than a decade of popping pills, I stuck my hand into the rays of sunlight and watched as the dust scattered and jumped around me. Everywhere, there was dirt, filth, and impurity, but I could not see even a speck of it until the door opened and the light came streaming in. Immediately, the light grabbed the filth and held up the impurity for me to see.

I was amazed at the conditions surrounding me. I had been living in this mess for years, but not until this very moment did I realize how the dust had owned me. The rays exposed the air that was full of grime. It was one of the toughest seasons of my life; I had to surrender to the belief that God would clean up the atmosphere because I finally knew I was incapable.

I was almost thirty-three. I had an array of drugs in different types, shapes, and colors. I had one to make me strong, one to make me happy, one to make me sleep, and one to wake me up. All I was missing was the White Rabbit and her "muchness."[1] The remedies would run out of the bottle and out of my system. They never lasted; they never healed anything.

I realized that the drugs were temporary at best; the more I took them, the more I found myself habituating to the dose. More pills were necessary to obtain the same level of manufactured peace. The vicious cycle had me trapped. I wanted out, even if it meant total defenselessness. My habit was getting dangerous and difficult. That is how sin functions; the slope of our sin gets steeper and more slippery. In fact, my slope was giving way to a treacherous mudslide. There was not so much as a crag of rock on which to catch a foothold.

I accepted my pain and was familiar with my specific level of hurt. I was not familiar with the hurt of the unknown, but I resolved to believe it could not be worse than this. This revelation made me aware and willing. Spiritually speaking, I was free of drugs in that moment of surrender! As is true of prayer, everything happens in the spiritual realm first; then, it manifests here on earth in the natural realm.

We will always be able to acknowledge a specific moment, a mere millisecond of time in which the transformation began. So often, the "fog of war" obscures these tiny but important details and accomplishments, but we need to recognize them.

Surrender is one of those very precious moments. I believe angels stop and dance for us when the healing begins. They sing. They laugh for our freedom because they see our futures with hope and purpose arriving. God smiles down on us and utters the words, "My good and faithful servant" (Matthew 25:21). In that instant, we release our will so that His will can be done (Matthew 6:10).

In my moment of surrender, I was physically sick. I weighed nowhere near what I should have weighed. I was a faint shade of green and unable to sleep for months after taking my last pill. Instead of sleeping, I would read my Bible and stare at the walls. I was not sure which words, if any, were sinking into the abyss that was my mind.

I was the most vulnerable I had ever been in my life so far. I had opened the door and placed my toes at the edge of the threshold, waiting for God

---

1   Lewis Carroll, *Alice in Wonderland.*

to gently lift me up and set me on His side. I was too tired and too vacant to move on my own.

All I could do was pray. It was enough; the Lord gave me His hand to hold. He had scheduled a divine appointment for me. On that particular day, I managed to get dressed and meet with a woman who had played tennis with me for years. I paid little attention to the fact that her husband was a pastor. I just knew she had something that I needed.

That day, I wore a tennis dress that fit perfectly several weeks prior; now, it looked like a sack on me. My stomach felt raw, and my nerves were jittery. I was cold and sweating at the same time. I spent a lot of money. When the pills did not fill the emptiness, I tried to fill it with stuff. I needed help fast. I had decided to stop taking the pills, and when I did, the reality of my condition and guilt came rushing in. I wanted to get better but had no idea what was next. I was scared.

In my fear, I turned to God, and He sent me a saint. She did not look down on me from her sainthood. She was with me and for me for no apparent reason. She allowed Christ in her to see me through His blood. We talked for hours. Her counsel was biblical and godly. She housed the Spirit and served the Lord, so she was obedient to interrupt her schedule to do His work. She told me to whisper the name above all names, and then she prayed for me.

Whispering was all I could do. Jesus was doing miraculous things in my life, but I was not quite seeing them yet. I stood in a dense fog at that moment with only hope, faith, and prayer.

If you are diligently pursuing Christ, and you feel like you are not doing much, He is doing things you are not capable or aware of, so keep allowing Him to sculpt. Our allowing God and others to help, pray for us, and see our surrender is another one of those moments where we deepen our friendship and trust with the Lord.

In my most vulnerable hour, I got godly advice because I chose to pray, seek, and surrender. In allowing only God to lead, I not only received advice, I received healing because God's answer trumps every request. Not only did that woman pray and believe for me, but her husband became my pastor years later. Only God can ordain such an umbrella of blessing.

She walked in Christ's likeness in order to walk me to Christ. I whispered, "Jesus," to get up, to get to meetings, and to take a shower. Sometimes, I asked Him to help me breathe. I replaced my pills with that name.

God picked me up, held me for a time, and was about to move me across the threshold of my surrender. I remember during this period being very aware that I was resting in the arms of the Lord. During this time, my Jesus placed me in a Christian treatment center. I spent months there. Do you remember the room I described at the beginning of my healing, the one with the circle of chairs and only a lamp? It was in this facility.

Being in treatment was not easy. Believing for the strength to get dressed and go to meetings was not easy. We cannot expect healing to be easy. Healing is good, hard, laborious work that will reap great rewards. The choice remains ours: we can allow or block God from handing us our healing and our blessings. We have free will. We need to surrender to God's will and ask Him in prayer to make His will ours.

Please do not give up. I did not. I did, however, cry at times. I missed my children. My emotions were strained. The tunnel looked long and dark, but funny thing I realized after passing through was only a half-foot door casing. By the grace of God and through faith, I stood, I stepped, and I trusted. It was so worth it!

Surrendered as I was, I looked like a deer in the headlights of life. I had never experienced life sober. I had always resorted to the escape hatch. The devil kept telling me to go back. I had spent a lifetime believing that avoiding surrender meant avoiding pain and hurt. That is the way of the enemy; he deceives us into believing the exact opposite of God's truth.

Take Heed What You Hear

We must be careful because satan does not want us to get better. He will tell us that because we have not conquered all the steps or all the issues, we need to give up. He suggests that there are too many steps or the journey is too hard. I was unaware at the time that the enemy was planting this advice in my mind. Nor did I realize that I was the one letting him enter. When I refused to listen to the lies, the enemy's scheme in certain areas was finished. God replaced the devil's lies with His truth.

I still had not surrendered a few areas of my life; I gave quite a foothold to the devil. How I related to my first marriage was one of those areas. It was a rollercoaster of a journey. I felt very vulnerable as I journeyed down and then up for many years. Scriptures like Colossians 3:18 (NIV), "Wives, submit to your husband, as is fitting in the Lord," left me feeling defeated; he was not like Christ to me.

The counselors at the treatment facility told me to move out and separate from my first husband. When we are healing, we are vulnerable and, many times, can only take so much at once.

This emotional state lends itself to the acceptance of bad things because we feel we cannot conquer the issues all at once—overload! In some cases, the advice of the enemy is cloaked in an angel-of-light costume. It is an effective maskquerade, and even though I successfully left, I went right back to believing the lies for fear of losing my children first and being alone in my newfound healing.

Make no mistake, the decision was ultimately mine; the problem was that I lacked a sound foundation from which to pull good instruction. During the healing process, the right guidance is critical to stick to. The discernment you need comes by surrendering only to God and through prayer. He tells us He will never give us more than we can handle, but we don't believe it. Can you accurately choose whom you should listen to and whom you should shut down? If you are uncertain, pray.

Before my infilling and during my vulnerable post-treatment state, I attempted to separate from my first husband. The fighting that ensued in the midst of that much pain was intolerable. Because I thought my children would suffer, I thought I had to go back. Sadly, I was exchanging one kind of control for another: the control of my environment once again. The kids probably suffered worse than if I stayed gone, with one exception: a beautiful baby girl was born during the following years, which made all the pain worth everything.

My first husband was hurting me still, and it was awful. Ridiculous as it sounds, I wanted to fix him. Of course, I could not even get myself together. I was stubborn about letting God do the work. (Are you trying to fix someone?)

Thankfully, God never gave up on me, and with His help, I eventually surrendered my crumbling marriage; I did it kicking and screaming, but I did it. That was when I began to heal in this regard; both my foundation and my fear began to slowly (it's a process) dissipate, and my life began to take the shape God intended. The devil had parts of my heart so hardened that I could not see the light in those areas.

Because of my surrender, faith, and prayers, my Jesus heard me and blessed me with the right voice, and the devil lost in that regard finally. However, the ten years of litigation and pain were almost unbearable, but oddly enough, I made it through those also. God is forever helping us upward.

God never leaves us nor forsakes us during our trials (Hebrews 13:5); we often leave or ignore Him, but He never leaves us. Jesus fought for me. He eventually gave me a new husband—one that emulates Christ, drawing me that much closer to knowing my God through his obedience, faith, and love.

Keep Up Your Spiritual Guard

Wholeness is a lifelong journey of warfare and resting in God. The enemy operates cyclically, cleverly repeating and morphing old patterns to keep us in bondage. When we get freedom in one area, he tries his tricks in another. He did the same with Jesus. When satan left Jesus in the desert, he did not leave for good. He planned to return at a more opportune time (Luke 4:13). Stand guard and allow God to fight for you!

We are conceding control to God. By allowing Him to remove the roots of sin and replant His seed in the soil of our hearts, we will make sure that God is the protector and healer in our lives. The denial we once accommodated was a hardening agent that made our hearts impervious to God. With denial left behind, our hearts become more pliable and open to Him.

We have relinquished control and entered into surrender, which we are mastering. We are allowing Him in to heal our hearts and souls. The reason people remain in bondage is that they stop surrendering. Upon salvation, we recognize our need for Christ. Sometimes, at this point, we are not yet mature enough to see our deeper needs and God's corresponding provision. It is okay to walk with Him for a while before we see the contrast between His ways and ours. In time, we realize our need for a deeper level of commitment and surrender.

We need all the provision God offers as we travel through His healing steps! Often, the process will dictate the need for others to nurture us and help us along. That is not always comfortable for us. Yet we cannot skip over His provision; it would be akin to turning around and walking back down the stairway or stopping mid-flight.

Often, we are too embarrassed to share with others or too busy to take the time to remove the masks. Then again, the things of God take effort and vulnerability; they always seem to rub against the grain of our comfort level. We are flesh and bones. He is spirit and truth. Let us remember to do things His way.

The next step is imperative. God will not let us graduate to higher levels until we walk out of the step we are on. The process becomes more natural the more we adhere to His leading. There may be some pauses, but the path upward is becoming smooth.

Take the most from what He is teaching you. Take a look around; assess the areas in which you are receiving healing and those in which surrender is not yet complete.

Congratulations! You have successfully made it up one more step. By releasing control, you have allowed surrender. This is a good place to be because, until you are truly surrendered, you are not truly free to be healed. He will never trespass against your free will. But you have surrendered, so stand ready to receive healing, blessings, gifts, and, best of all, His love.

You have also added a new awareness: prayer! You are getting ready to experience a new level of freedom and joy. Soon, you will know a new level of His liberty; it is what I call passing from the know into the flow—the place where you understand the Scripture that says His burden is light and His yoke is easy (Matthew 11:28).

Keep truckin'; expect His angels to rally and dispense His will in His perfect time. You are doing a great job and stepping into a healthy life. Take that mask off, take a deep breath, and step up!

CHAPTER FOUR

THE THRONE OF SUPREME COUNSEL

STEP FOUR: GODLY GUIDANCE BY HIS WORD

"You guide me with Your counsel,
and afterward You will take me into glory"

(Psalm 73:24, NIV)

The threshold you are about to cross is the acceptance of godly guidance. As you cross it, you allow fresh air to envelop you. You are finally ready to greet your guest, your God-ordained guide, The Word of God. This will also increase your measure of faith because we gain faith by Scripture.

Let us recount our current position: We have stopped denying the existence of our imperfections and control issues. We are no longer hiding without hope behind the closed door with the open latch. We are faithfully surrendered and have prayerfully arrived at the perfect time and place to seek a hand to hold.

Once the door is open and the threshold is exposed to view, we pray for our healing and pass through the door at will. The door is open. We welcome help into our hearts and stop hiding.

This is a place where individual accountability and responsibility for our healing are critical. Our independence to this point has served a purpose. It has allowed us to build relationship and trust with God alone. We learned to accept our responsibility without blaming others. We know that He alone is enough.

Humans naturally tend to glorify earthly counsel or counselors. It is important to remember that they are only willing vessels; this helps us to praise God and thank Him for the ability of these people to exhibit the love that comes from Him. When we understand the source of their goodness toward us, we can receive what He offers through their participation.

Our awareness for this step is reading. Understanding our responsibility to read God's Word helps us to own and discern the godly guidance He provides. When we meditate on His Word, we find our daily bread and our sword of protection. It was too early to dictate a full read of scripture prior to this step, but you are ready now, and you will find that this will strengthen the awareness you gained on prior steps. You will find that you may now grow exponentially because it is His Word that ignites depth of faith.

God tells us in Romans 10:17 that faith comes through hearing His Word. His Word is truly a powerful weapon (Hebrews 4:12)! Proverbs 30:5 (NIV) says, "Every word of God is flawless; He is a shield to those who take refuge in Him." We come to Him as little children. Children are flexible, open, and hungry for truth; they are the perfect example of openness to guidance.

Our prayer for faith every morning increases our gift of faith. Hearing God is what strengthens us, although we might not realize it immediately. I did not realize the magnificent power of what my daily dose was doing until years later.

Remember, when you are hurting, it is normal to feel weary, overwhelmed, or unsure about what you are gaining when you read the Bible. You are not alone in questioning the meaning of Scripture. He tells us clearly that it is a mystery until we are converted (Colossians 1:26). Did you know that one of the devil's favorite tactics is to make you feel overwhelmed or confused when you read Scripture?

We step into the Word the same way we do anything with God, the very way we have stepped into healing so far. First, we get rid of doubt. We dismiss the fear of not understanding, and we choose to reside in faith. Daily doses of the Bible, preferably three or more chapters each day, provide protection for the journey. Three chapters a day keeps the devil away! (See the chart at the end of the book.)

Heaven's "Medicine"

Take small doses of Scripture at first. Read just a verse, a parable, or a chapter. If you are having a hard time understanding, pray that God will interpret the message He wants you to receive. Slow down and rest as you read, believing there is power in the intake. Our reading serves as medicine for an empty soul, healing every part of the mind and heart. As we progress, we move from the simplest truths (the milk of the Word) to the meat of deep revelatory meaning (see 1 Corinthians 3:2; Hebrews. 5:12; 1 Peter 2:2).

Hearing and reading His Word will combat the enemy's attempts to keep us sick and vulnerable to the wrong things and people. Through our reading, God will teach us to discern godly versus ungodly advice. Not all secular advice is bad, but all secular advice that fails to line up with God's heart is bad. The words may sound innocent or even kind, but so did the devil's spouting of Scripture in the desert with Jesus (Matthew 4:6; Psalm 91:11–12).

Jesus was not fooled by the desert battle of biblical poetry and law. He saw how the devil's wrong motives were couched in what seemed to be the right words. Jesus responded with Scripture but without manipulating its meaning. He quoted Deuteronomy 8:3 (NIV): "Man does not live on bread alone but on every word that comes from the mouth of God." He also quoted Psalm 78:18, 41, and 56, reminding the devil of the dangers of putting God to the test.

Let us pray always for the meaning in the Word—the manna or substances of it, the life within it—to fill our minds and hearts. We pray for God to speak to us through His Word, that the scriptures would guard us, and that we would remember what we read, never allowing it to be stolen from us (Matthew 13:19). We implore that the Word be transformed from logos (divine words), into rhema (life-giving power).

As you continue in the Word of God, stop and consider the following questions: How has God's Word offered you hope during tough times? Do you have faith that He will help you understand it as you read?

Ask Him for the desire to read the Bible daily, craving it more than you crave TV and fruitless desires. He is our hope. He is our healing. Only to Him and His Word can we be safely surrendered. The Word precedes the foundations of the earth! John 1:1 says (NIV), "In the beginning was the Word, and the Word was with God, and the Word was God." His Word is everlasting!

Notice that prayer and Scripture are part of every step from now on. If you need to refer to earlier steps again, always take prayer and Scripture with you.

Counsel and Truth

Paul warned: "Do not be misled. 'Bad company corrupts good character'" (1 Corinthians 15:33, NIV). Accountability and help from the right people are important in the healing process. God is our ultimate authority; He has fashioned us to love and balance one another. "As iron sharpens iron, so a friend sharpens a friend" (Proverbs 27:17, NLT). You might need some new friends. You might even need to separate yourself from some extended family members at this point (Matthew 10:34–39). To keep stepping upward in our journey, we must travel with those who are willing to do the same.

Paul instructed his spiritual "son" Titus to separate himself from ungodly counsel:

But avoid foolish controversies and genealogies and arguments and quarrels about the law because these are unprofitable and useless. Warn a divisive person once, and then warn him a second time. After that, have nothing to do with him. You may be sure that such a man is warped and sinful; he is self-condemned

(Titus 3:9–11)

During my less-than-honorable years, I found that the resolution of my pain was not to be found in the counsel of man. The right counsel would come directly from God or from God through a discernible man. I learned that "It is better to take refuge in the Lord than to trust in man" (Psalm 118:8).

Man without God is in the business of fixing things by way of his own understanding. Scripture clearly states that we are not to lean on our own understanding (Proverbs 3:5). All the twelve-step programs, books, and methods are only temporary fixes if they do not lead us to the power Christ Jesus offers us. The only way to be permanently healed is to experience God. He is the only one who can set us free (John 8:36).

Some of the best, most professional earthly counsel I received came from those who worked according to their own ability, and their best was not sufficient. They gave advice regardless of their lack of biblical knowledge, godly experience, and life experience. It seemed as though many of them were in denial themselves. The true healing method was of no interest to them. Most had not experienced anything close to what I had been through. They had not walked the dark alleys I had walked. They matured while safely tucked away in university libraries. Their well-worn library cards and psycho jargon were not helping me.

I became numb to the counseling "system." I chose to deny the ability of the counselors I was seeking. Fear and unbelief kept me there. I had convinced myself that because no one had helped me thus far, no one could help. Every time I entered a new office, I would divide the hours into quarters and count how many times the counselor used the terms cognitive, inferiority complex, relational stability, behavioral accountability, and medicine. I cannot remember them using the term the blood of Christ—that is the very reason I use my degree and practice to profess Christ when applicable in word but always in prayer.

Genuine guidance comes when God directs the vessel. Most often, we seek guidance when we feel bad emotionally and are vulnerable. Many times, we do not even realize we are in the wrong office. This is dangerous ground.

The pursuit of godly counsel is just as important as coming out of denial, releasing control, and stepping into surrender. If we are to move forward, we need a system of accountability that is based in Christ. We need to allow godly counselors to know us. That does not mean that we are comfortable with their knowing us. But if God has sent God-fearing, trustworthy ministers to help us, they need to know the good, the bad, and the really bad parts of our lives. What we keep hidden will keep us in bondage.

In other words, if I have not stepped up the stairway into healing from their particular issue, I tell the person seeking counsel in that area that I am sorry for their struggle and will pray for them. If my counsel is sought by a woman who feels trapped in an abusive marriage, drug addiction, addiction, grief, or anxiety, I will take her hand and walk all the stairs with her as God leads.

When I was in trouble, I needed someone who had actually walked in and out of shadowy corners—someone who would not fear going into the dark rooms to help me retrieve parts of my heart and soul. I needed someone who had actually been to war. A degree qualifies someone by man's measure. In my life, man's measuring device was powerless, at best.

Of course, I understand that research, study, and knowledge are tremendous blessings. I am not discounting them; they serve us well. In the end, however, doctrine without the Spirit and love of God will leave you feeling incomplete, sometimes to the point of destruction.

By way of much prayer, I try not to seek in a textbook what I should be seeking in His Word or at His well. In John chapter 4, while sitting at Jacob's well in the heat of the noonday sun, Jesus offered the Samaritan woman living water. He explained that if we come to God's will, we will never thirst again (John 4:4–13).

In our flesh, we idolize things and people according to standards that are not God's. We esteem worldly knowledge and leave little room for God. In Jesus' day, the counsel of the Pharisees and Sadducees was killing people. Why? Because the center of healing is not man's theory; it is God's truth. If we base our hopes for healing in worldly hypotheses, we should not then wonder why our healing does not last.

Meditate at the Right Well

"Hurry, hurry, kids! Hurry up!" I yelled. "Come out to the backyard fast. There is an owl in our tree, and he is staring at me!"

I hollered up the winding staircase, hopeful the message made it around all the corners.

God sent us an owl that literally took up residence in the oak tree in our backyard. He stayed for several weeks and would watch us, not like an owl, but like a hawk. We were clueless at the time, but five years later, wisdom and God-fearing counsel arrived.

God was letting us know what was ahead. Watch your surroundings. God can use anything He chooses to keep you on track and point you to the promise of blessings to come.

> *Blessed is the man who does not walk in the counsel of the wicked, stand in the way of sinners, or sit in the seat of mockers. But his delight is in the law of the Lord, and on His law he meditates day and night*
>
> (Psalm 1:1–2)

God creates many opportunities for wise counsel for those who are attentive to what He is doing in their lives. Likewise, the enemy offers many "wells" of ungodly counsel. Where are you spending your time? What are you reading and watching? How are your indulgences helping in your healing? Whom do you revere? Why do you respect them?

What may seem to be my opinion at times is actually based in truth concerning the condition of our fallen world (2 Timothy 3:1–9). Too often, we seek answers from a dry well, an evil structure that is void of truth. Without the counsel of Christ (John 14:16) that is poured out for all, no true healing can occur.

You may find something appealing, something that looks like healing. Things may look better for a while, but what is really happening? Remember that deception has to look appealing enough to get you hooked. Then the mask comes off, and the real game is on, and probably again.

Just like the masses, I claimed to want healing. What I really wanted was my way and to be around enablers who would pay attention to me and provide an excuse to continue in my sickness. I was the one who was going to the wrong well. Whether we find it because of a lack of knowledge or a sense of trepidation, the wrong well will poison us.

That is why, with God as our guide, we have stepped out of ignorance and fear. We choose to surround ourselves with godly guidance: pastors, mentors, friends, church family, and God-fearing counselors. The newfound strength and faith that we are building through our healing allows us to accept our imperfections. We realize we are not and cannot be perfect; Christ is perfect. Our character is not in our ability. Our distinctiveness is found in His ability to work through us by His Spirit.

Through prayer and godly communication, we are connecting with others who know which well is the right one. James said, "Confess your sins to each other and pray for each other so that you may be healed. The prayer of a righteous man is powerful and effective" (James 5:16, NLT).

We are positioned to make progress, in part because we are ready to come clean where sin is concerned. Proverbs 28:13 warns, "He who conceals his sins does not prosper, but whoever confesses and renounces them finds mercy." You will find that when you disclose your sin issues to a God-fearing vessel, he or she will pray for you. In time and with your submission to God's guidance, you will find relief.

Try not to keep secrets; the devil loves to manipulate us with hidden stuff. This is the very reason why guidance is so important. When you have an ear to hear true wisdom, you are not looking for attention or pity. You are looking for prayer and healing; you want to be well. When your identity is in Christ, you are free to be yourself without condemnation. Suddenly, you can handle constructive criticism and welcome genuine guidance. Your craving for empty words of flattery disappears.

When you desire wisdom from the right well, you are satisfied to hear from God. You no longer need approval or affirmation from man. Instead of trying to get agreement through gossip or manipulation, you find peace from God through prayer. The only intermediary you need is Christ.

Do you have good counsel right now? If not, will you stop, open your Bible, and read a Scripture regarding counsel? Will you ask God in prayer to send you help? Feeling overwhelmed is okay, but please keep stepping upward. It is fine to feel unsure about this new territory. Just trust that your feet are on holy ground and you are blessed.

Jesus Is Our Guide

What results in deliverance and healing is for the counselor to have been through more than the sick person. The One who always fits that bill is Jesus. We can look to His cross because He suffered it all. He is the Healer, Jehovah Rapha (Exodus 15:26).

Let us take another step into healing and another step closer to our godly purpose in this life. If the steps seem impossible to accomplish in your own strength, then you know we are right on track.

God's plan is underway. He is working in and through us. "For we are God's workmanship, created in Christ Jesus to do good works, which God prepared in advance for us to do" (Ephesians 2:10, NIV). This is not the time to quit; it is the time to press on!

You are loved and purposed for greatness. Keep stepping and demasking. You will see. I promise. I did not believe it until I stepped it out, either, but His healing is true. Remember to read your Bible. That is our awareness for this step. We need to read The Guidebook in order to stay healthy on our trip. Let us pray and ask The Lord to help us find proper godly guidance with a pure heart.

Keep these words: "A wise man has great power, and a man of knowledge increases strength; for waging war, you need guidance..." (Proverbs 24:5–6, NHEB) Our travels will not be easy, but they will be blessed, and we will not be traveling alone. We will now move on to the next step: stopping the cycle of the enemy. I always compare this to pulling weeds out of my yard, especially after a dry season when the ground is hard and impossible.

The weeds' gestation cycles are inevitable. Every year at the same time, the same types manifest in clusters. The hardened soil holds the offending root firmly in place. Pulling it out is hard work. But after a good rain, the ground is soft and pliable, and the root comes right up.

We have to open up and allow God to pour out His rain, His cleansing, His power, and His covering. A softened heart will accept His ways. Surrendering to His guidance is what we need to ensure God's removal of the roots and the restoration of our souls.

An example of this power is in Philippians chapter 4. This chapter guides us as to how to combat fear. It was written to two women in the church, Euodia and Syntyche, who are misbehaving. Paul had to guide them back into proper fellowship. Notice how he shepherds them in love. Godly guidance is so important. We also learn from this passage that praise/worship and gentleness guide us into peace.

For now, congratulations! You have accepted godly guidance. You have also added a new awareness: reading His Word! You are healing, and God sees your diligence. You will not give up. You are climbing higher into a healthy life, tossing off masks left and right, never to be touched again.

Take another step up!

CHAPTER FIVE

UNMASK THE CYCLE OF DEFEAT

STEP FIVE: WORSHIP CEASES THE CYCLING

"Trust in the Lord with all your heart and lean not on your own understanding; in all your ways acknowledge Him, and He will make your paths straight"

(Proverbs 3:5–6, NIV, emphasis mine)

You have stepped up so far that you might feel overwhelmed. If so, rest in God's command: "Be still and know that I am God..." (Psalm 46:10, NIV) Be still and focus on Him. Allow your healing to settle in, and praise Him for who He is.

Remember that God's healing takes time; there is no set calendar. Remember, you are healing and moving progressively toward blessing; it rarely manifests as fast as you expect it to. Just keep standing, and keep up the good work. Take Paul's advice from Thessalonians 3:13: "As for you...never tire of doing what is right."

Look down at your feet and realize they have been stepping for and toward Him this whole time. We are moving toward awareness, breaking cycles of abuse, and pulling up bad roots. We have come so far! Every prior step was necessary to get to these higher ones. Do you feel good about what you have accomplished? You should. You have put effort into healing, and God sees your heart.

Remember to deflect the devil's lies with the truth in your reading and praying. That, too, is a form of worship. The enemy knows exactly which buttons to push. He waits until you are weak or have let your guard down; then he pushes them. I know because I kept falling into the same cycle. Every time I failed, it felt like I got the results I deserved instead of the ones I wanted.

The irony is that, even so, I was shocked at the results. The definition of insanity is doing the same thing repeatedly but expecting different results. Some of that was evident in my approach! Our best defense is a consistent offense: continuous stepping up on the staircase of healing to combat the devil's cycle of bondage.

Where do you see repetitive behaviors in your life? What harm are these behaviors causing? Do you want to stop? Do you feel powerless over the pain? If you answered yes to any of the last three questions, then boldly step up and let God stop the pain. If it is a new revelatory issue, don't be afraid to start over at the first step with each new awareness of bondage. God works in a multitude of ways; once you are healed from one issue, He may surface more that we can be healed of!

Let me explain further. God tells us in Genesis that every inclination of man's heart is toward evil (Genesis 6:5). That is our fleshly nature. You can see the iniquity historically. Every dispensation has ended in apostasy due to man's sinful nature. If we do not step in tune with the Spirit and crucify our flesh, we will act and react in fleshly ways. Not only is the human character marred, but our hearts and souls are not whole. We need to allow God to fix both.

When we notice the same arguments, problems, habits, and issues arising day in and day out, we know the devil has us in a cycle of bondage. We must allow God to stop the escalator in satan's funhouse so that we can step off and into God's arms. He will then help us go back in our memories to find the origin of the pain.

Pain fragments portions of our hearts and souls, making us vulnerable. The devil then captures and guards our fragments with gatekeepers such as denial, control, pride, anger, etc. These gatekeepers are the things that we have been working to dismantle/unmask in previous chapters. Once we are aware of their role and realize they are not working for our good, God can go in and preside over our territory. Give Him providence over your heart and soul.

Restoration is the very reason the fullness of God's Holy Spirit is necessary. We are incapable of restoring our hearts and souls without Him. With Him, we can restore anything willing. Even in the midst of our pain, we will begin to worship Him, our awareness for this step. He inhabits our praise.

We need His transforming presence to heal and stop the cycle of our pain (2 Corinthians 3:18). We can usher Him in through our adoration; in His presence, He heals us. We are going to cover some basic housecleaning rules in order to purify ourselves for worship. Then, we are going to learn to praise Him.

Awareness of the Cycle

The cycles of healing become obvious when you examine them with spiritual eyes. Awareness is a must as you climb the stairs to freedom. Thus far, our awareness has brought us from hope to faith, to prayer, to reading Scripture consistently, and to worship/praise!

Maintain constant awareness, knowing your surroundings either glorify God or satan. Historically, presently, and prophetically, society is tilted against the Body of Christ. There is always the call to fight the good fight, both for what is going on internally and what is going on around you. Pray with discernment, asking God to expose the evil order and its cycles.

It is time to end the cycle of unhealthy behaviors, emotions, and environments. God will help us prevail through supernatural warfare. The psalmist encourages us to be open to God's scrutiny, knowing that His motives are pure: "Put me on trial, Lord, and cross-examine me. Test my motives and my heart. For I am always aware of Your unfailing love, and I have lived according to Your truth" (Psalm 26:2–3, NLT).

With so many issues in our lives being confronted, we may be amazed at the peace that we find in the process. Often, when the process slows down or God momentarily refrains from raising any new red flags, we assume that our healing is finished. We are never finished as long as we are still stepping on this planet. We are, however, unmasked and moving upward toward freedom!

Satan comes to steal, kill, and destroy (John 10:10). Just as is true in The Masquerade, where the stairs cycle endlessly downward, we tend to revolve around our pain. He will keep us spinning in the same sick patterns as long as we allow it. Right now, we are going to learn how to interrupt his cycles.

Unearthing Old Roots

I got off the phone with my father. Another year had gone by without a visit from him. We got along well, and I just refused to accept his avoidance. He didn't care too much for my marital choice. Bailing my first husband out of jail and out of bookies had cost him endless amounts of worry and money.

He would rather stay away, I guessed as I swallowed another pill to blunt the pain of inadequacy and rejection.

I had poor coping mechanisms for my immediate pain, but in reality, the source of this pain was the childhood abandonment I felt when my parents divorced. Feeling abandoned and abused again in adulthood reinforced the negative cycle and also pressed to keep me in a dysfunctional marriage. Distancing was part of my father's way of dealing with difficulty.

My father was not the real issue: I loved him dearly, and he loved me. However, his decisions may have been the initial catalyst for some of my pain, but I was the only one who could resolve that within me. I needed to put the pill bottle down, track back to the original hurt, the root, and ask God to help me.

On our current step, we come to grips with vicious cycles and gain understanding of the embedded patterns that support our sickness. This is also the step where we allow God to eliminate the cycles implemented by satan to protect the bad roots in our lives. These take work to uncover because the devil installs gatekeepers to stand guard over these roots.

Over time, our habits and behaviors develop around the issues and cycles that plague us. Our reactions form patterns that bring us deeper under the control of evil.

Alone, we are incapable of removing these issues. It is difficult to uncover the depths to which roots become implanted or the time and place when habitual cycles began. Without God, a root is impossible to remove. But once we allow Him to reveal the reason behind the pain (and if we surrender with forgiveness), He will take the pain away forever. God must be the gardener here.

Once again, it is imperative that we cry out for God's fullness in us. We must be able to tap into something larger than ourselves in order to access the resources needed to do the work. The resources are divine; only divinity can combat this type of evil order. We have given the devil freedom to till the ground of our souls for so long that he has established colonies of demons and instituted the bad habits they bring. We need holy hands to wield the shovel, unearth the roots, and overthrow the cycles of hell.

When a plant takes root, it produces successive harvests of fruit. There are battles that we fight over and over again because the root is intact under the soil and may have been for generations. We cannot see the root, but it guides us into the same arguments, the same offenses, the same hurt feelings, time after time. It reminds me of the way children act. They remember the last altercation with their siblings, and they pick up where they left off. Here is an example from our home:

"He got the front seat last time!" she whines.

"She did, and she called me dumb and pushed me," he retaliates.

Then comes the crying and, in our house, the inevitable rebuke and sometimes spanking. I will not listen to the quarreling.

From the outside looking in, the cycle looks ignorant. Yet, I confess that my first husband and I did not act much differently when we would argue. We think our children's spats are silly, but ours are no better. It is what I call "plank-in-eye syndrome." We see the flecks in other people's eyes but fail to see the telephone poles sticking out of our own (Matthew 7:4).

More dangerous than our judgments is our ignorance of our own cycles. If we remain ignorant, the spinning continues, arguments or no arguments. Our stance needs to be: "As for me and my household, we will serve the LORD" (Joshua 24:15, NIV). Serving the Lord is about what you do; it is about your reverence and regard for Him. Cycles and roots are combated in worship as God's love penetrates our hate.

About two years after my "thirty-three-year-old experience with God," I became aware of the cycles in my life. You may be shaking your head and wondering how I could be so "asleep at the wheel" after having access to the Holy Spirit all that time. The truth is that healing is something we cannot rush. I had stepped into sobriety and was learning how to live sober. The idea of a healthy life was just sinking in. God was preparing me for the higher steps.

We always have to be ready for God to break us down, clean us up, and make us aware. Then, we have to let God ready us again. This succession is a linear flow of hope. God's truth will replace the sick cycle that has kept us hurting so long. Satan operates in a similar but contrary way; he replicates and counterfeits God's order in an attempt to destroy our destinies, essentially flipping the script.

The roots were working in my life. I kept seeing the same arguments, and I was sick of them. Sometimes, we are too tired to fight; sometimes, we are just too tired to do anything about it all while too scared. Neither circumstance applied in my case, so I prayed, stood, believed with faith, and fought all this on one step. I felt like I was beating my head into a brick wall repeatedly. I would watch the same demonic cycles resurface, and I would react in godly ways. Weeks later, the same evil mess would crop up again.

"What on earth?" My shout came from a heart so passionately trying and yet so desperately failing. My question answered itself. The earth is satan's turf; he is manipulating the logistics around here.

Yet, we have protection. Our protection just happens to be where the real battle is raging—in the heavenly realms. We rarely travel far enough in our hearts and minds to realize it. But we need to go there, and we need to take the right road: we will wage war in worship.

The Realm of Battle

Through worship, we enter the field on which the battle is being waged. We elevate our awareness to the spiritual realm, where we can arm ourselves with effective weapons designed to defeat our real enemy—satan. Paul described the realm of battle beautifully:

Finally, be strong in the Lord and in His mighty power. Put on the full armor of God, so that you can take your stand against the devil's schemes. For our struggle is not against flesh and blood, but against the rulers, against the authorities, against the powers of this dark world and against the spiritual forces of evil in the heavenly realms.

Ephesians 6:10–12 (NIV)

When an argument arises in my life, I have to remind myself that I am not arguing with that issue; I am arguing with the cycles I have allowed satan to implement in my life. I need to rise above the physical details and not glorify the drama. When we rise above the physical level, we know that we are growing spiritually. We are stepping higher and getting closer to God. There, we reside in the heavenly realms with praise. This upward mobility puts our weapons, purpose, protection, and healing within reach.

This does not mean we will never again be tempted to fight in the flesh. We will always be tempted to do so. We can, however, raise our chances of nipping temptation in the bud.

I remember a night when the room was dark, and I was almost asleep. I was scheduled to speak at a community worship service that next night. I was prayed up and prepared to minister, but I was not ready for the warfare that was about to erupt. The most ridiculous part of this story is that satan did not even need to use a new technique to get this thing going. No, the devil dipped into the same old cycle; familiar words came out of my first husband's mouth.

As usual, disruption! He fought all night, which was commonplace. To this day, I could not even offer a reason for the fight, whether it was satan's attempt to make me feel unworthy and keep me quiet. The drama never would cease with him. I know this much: I wasted a good night's sleep and allowed my joy to be stolen.

The speech went over without a hitch. By that time, I was totally dependent upon God to carry me; all I could do was let Him speak through me (which is the only way to speak for God anyhow).

You reside in the heavenly realms above these battles of the flesh. Rise up! It took me way too long to realize God never intended this power struggle with satan. What many call warfare is merely a lack of spiritual conditioning and a deficiency in knowledge of their placement in the Kingdom.

Dig deep and notice any repetitive behaviors that make you sad, fearful, or angry. Even after years of healing, one of mine was the inability to shut down the abuse coming at me and fight the right way by exiting. Find the cycles; look deep under the soil of your heart so that you can cut them loose and release them to God. The point where my cycle began to break was when my revelation came when I was finally surrendered.

Once we become determined to arrest the cycles in our lives, God steps in and gives us a place to rest in Him. He literally stopped me in my tracks. For a time, I felt like I was on hold or in slow motion. He had to slow me down so that the spinning top that was this cycle in my life could stop. When it did, I saw writing on it. It said, "Fear, fear, fear, rejection, shame, and abandonment." That was what I needed to know and be healed from so that I could exit the cycle.

Power and Peace

Worship is the central truth in this chapter. I believe it is no accident that the topic comes up near the center point of this book.

Praising God keeps us in a peaceful place of healing where we can grow steadily into Christ's likeness. Here we can love others from a godly perspective, alleviating a lot of our pain and protecting ourselves from further external hurts. We will also begin to learn who to walk away from and who to draw near to.

We are responsible for learning about the role of worship because God created us to worship Him. How powerful is the truth that satan himself headed up the praise team in heaven, and his current work of control is the very reason we are hurting down here? We need power, not control. Find that power and know that, just as satan's relationships sent him south of the third heaven, so do ours (Ezekiel 28).

As long as we are sick and hurting, why wouldn't our relationships be a mess? Our relationships reflect our own condition. Everyone is involved in some type of relationship, whether with friends, spouses, children, siblings, parents, coworkers, church members, or extended family. Whatever the relationships, each of us is aware of arguments and disagreements that follow cyclical patterns.

Once we enjoy internal freedom in Christ, the enemy will attack us through our associations. We must deny all of his attempts. As God broke down and destroyed my personal cycles (co-dependency to an awful marriage, addiction, depression, and anxiety), new hurts started coming in from the outside. Just as satan used other people to plant some of the original bitter roots in our lives, he will attempt to reestablish outside influences to inflict fresh pain. He sees that our healing has undermined his original plan, so he initiates new ones.

God's plan is for godly relationships on all levels. In the following passage from Ephesians, Paul addresses the Jews and the Gentiles. However, because the power of God's Word operates on multiple levels, I also see this passage as instructive to all godly unions: church and state, equally yoked marriage, sound relationships, etc.:

For He Himself is our peace, who has made the two one and has destroyed the barrier, the dividing wall of hostility, by abolishing in His flesh the law with its commandments and regulations. His purpose was to create

in Himself one new man out of the two, thus making peace, and in this
one body to reconcile both of them to God through the cross, by which He
put to death their hostility.

Ephesians 2:14–16 (NIV)

Baby Girl "Blue"

I sat up, bent over on the gurney, and pulled air and prayer into my body. I kept my head tilted toward the cross of Christ on the wall. I said His name aloud as the anesthetist inserted the epidural. "Jesus, my Jesus."

I felt the sting, and soon the medicine began to numb my toes. The anesthetist lowered me back down to the gurney and taped my arms straight out like the Messiah on the cross. My knees, my waist, and then my neck began to prickle and buzz. I thought how amazing it was that I could lie awake while a doctor literally cut open my body.

I rested in Christ.

"She's numb; we are ready," the doctor said with authority.

I took one last breath before he cut and lifted a prayer to heaven silently, "Please, Lord, have her be healthy. Do not let my sins affect her. Forgive me, Father, for my weakness and sickness; do not allow the pain to fall on her physically or mentally. Please have her be healthy."

The doctor touched my abdomen with the scalpel and applied pressure; the blade began to penetrate my flesh deeper and deeper.

"I can feel the knife. I can feel the pain. I can feel it, and—please—it hurts! Help me! Stop cutting me! Please!"

I could get no more words out before he inserted a tube into my throat. Suddenly, I was unaware of the precious birth that was about to occur. I felt I deserved the void. In all the commotion, they neglected to ask my first husband into the room. He could hear but not see what was going on.

That baby girl was born without her mommy or daddy's comforting greeting. We did not deserve her. God sometimes gives us gifts that we do not deserve because He knows we will eventually rise to the occasion.

I call our precious middle baby girl Blue, not because I spent years surrounding her birth literally in sickness and tears, but because our whole family has dark eyes, and she is the proud owner of two huge crystal-blue ones. Whenever I read the passage about Moses seeing God on Mount Sinai standing on blue sapphire, I think of my daughter's eyes.

So often, during times of great joy, warfare develops. I was most depressed and vulnerable to the devil and his cycles during this time period. The doctors had medicated me during my pregnancy; I was terrified that my child would be born sick. She was born alone but very healthy.

My sadness had nothing to do with my baby girl. She is perfect. My sadness was because the cycle was so evil. I felt like I could not break the fear and medication off my life. The spinning got worse before it got better. The cycle of addiction during those transitional years became almost unbearable. I could feel the pressure, and so could the enemy.

While, in reality, I was moving closer to freedom, everything seemed to be getting worse. I did not realize that my experience was common to those who are verging on a breakthrough. When you press through the pressure and get a glimpse of what God has in store, the devil knows that he is losing the reins on your life. Healing has arrived.

In what areas have you begun to recognize the evil cycle on your life? Are you ready to allow God to stop the spinning? If so, do you believe He will? Please do not forget to hope, have faith, pray always, read three chapters a day, and worship Him! Remember, worship takes us into a safe place where God protects us from everything and everyone.

Consistent Pressing into the Asphalt

Do you remember my purgatory stage as I crawled out of the hell of dependence back in chapter two? God literally split that year into two halves: six months of my own might and six months of baby steps in His Spirit, neatly divided by my infilling of the Holy Spirit.

That year started with the release of the pill bottles I held so tightly. After five months without pills and having just graduated from treatment, I separated from my first husband (unfortunately, I went back for seven more years), moved out of my home, and into an apartment. The abusive cycle in my marriage was too much for me.

I did not understand. So often, we don't. We are healing and making great changes, but the relationships surrounding us are often exactly what satan uses to draw us back into sickness. Relationships are part of life, and that is why we are covering associations on this step. While we are going through an individual healing process, we must be aware of our links to other people. I did not take this into account, and I went back to my first husband out of fear.

When we are sick, we need to accept the fact that our friends, spouse, family, and kids are having a rough time, too. Our hope lies in the fact that, just as God is healing us, He can heal our relationships. In my healing, He healed some friends and family and took some away from me. Either way, I had to surrender the cycle and them unto Him. Sometimes, following Christ means letting go of people and things we love. I finally got away from my first husband years later and have been free for over a decade. I was healing, but it was too much for me all at once. I will explain this conundrum as we step together:

> *Peter said to Him, "We have left everything to follow You!" "I tell you the truth," Jesus replied, "no one who has left home or brothers or sisters or mother or father or children or fields for Me and the gospel will fail to receive a hundred times as much in this present age...and in the age to come, eternal life.*

> Mark 10:28–30 (NIV)

Regardless of the pain and detriment my first marriage caused me, God still gave blessings: a physical manifestation of His promise, one that I could hold. I was sober, awake, and right there to welcome her. She is delightful, loving, and joyful. Her eyes sparkle, and she emanates peace. God has allowed me to see His pleasure even during so much pain. The love is beyond words. My other two children are just as much of a blessing. They are precious gifts from the throne room. I recognize the timing of Jordan's birth and realize that

I almost missed her, making my inability to handle removing all the masks at once all okay. Let us not miss our glory. God has it saved up in heaven, but He shows up down here in amazing ways.

Place of Praise

Take a look around; you are standing on higher ground. If you feel a tad dizzy, it is okay. I felt the same way. Denial and control have been released. We have stepped into surrender and guidance. We are protecting ourselves with constant prayer and the daily reading of the Word. We are aware of our relationships and recognize negative cycles.

On this step, we add the awareness of praise. If you are unsure as to how to praise and worship God, just put in a praise and worship CD. During this very step in my life, I received a book on shouting to the Lord. It actually asked me to stand in my living room and shout out praises to Him. I did what the book said. I found out that words work, especially when they are heartfelt cries!

He made us to extol Him. If we do not praise Him, the rocks will (Luke 19:40). When I have good news and call my Vicki D., she will say, "That is tambourine-shaking revelation." Get one, shake it, and jump up and down while singing, "Thank You, Jesus, for my healing!" I am not kidding. Better yet, go get you a shofar (if that is foreign to you, make it an indigenous blessing).

Get before Him with a humble and contrite heart with nothing but glory for Him. Remove thoughts and requests from your mind and heart. Ask forgiveness; enter His gates with thanksgiving and His courts with praise (Psalm 100:4). Ask Him to take you from the outer court into the Holy Place and then behind the torn curtain into the Holy of Holies. Then bask in His presence and might. Worship all the time and everywhere.

I have a prayer room in my home. Some days, I spend hours in that space dancing, singing, and thanking Him. People do that for football teams that have nothing invested in their lives once they leave the stadium. Why do we cap our excitement for and from God, who is willing to come into the same room as us upon the mention of His name? Lift Him up in worship and watch His presence fall. We need His presence to heal us, fix our families, and restore our surroundings. If we have relationships, we must honor those who are honorable and allow them to heal right alongside us and leave those who are not honorable.

Once we recognize the cycles that hinder us, we need to find the initial hurt, the root that generated the cycle in the first place. The next step is to allow God to destroy the root. This is how the cycle is broken. We become aware, and God Himself eradicates the underlying issue and restores that portion of the soul. Suddenly, we notice that we have stepped off the escalator, careening toward hell. Now, we are moving into a new cycle called hope.

> *So then, just as you received Christ Jesus as Lord, continue to live in Him, rooted and built up in Him, strengthened in the faith as you were taught, and overflowing with thankfulness. See to it that no one takes you captive through hollow and deceptive philosophy, which depends on human tradition and the basic principles of this world rather than on Christ*

> (Colossians 2:6–8)

Congratulations, you have successfully made it up another step. You are aware of the cycles in your life and are worshiping the Almighty God.

Step up, my healthy friend, and pull off another layer of masks!

Chapter Six

DEEP ROOTS IN ROYAL GROUND

Step Six: Excavate the Roots by Resting in Him

"They are like trees in autumn that are doubly dead, for they bear no fruit and have been pulled up by the roots"

(Jude 1:12, NLT)

Then Christ will make His home in your hearts as you trust in Him. Your roots will grow down into God's love and keep you strong

(Ephesians 3:17, NLT)

Well into my healing, I was disobedient, bitter, and angry. I had overcome a lot through Christ, yet, in some circumstances, I had released symptoms but not the root issue. Once we allow God to destroy the root, the nasty feelings begin to subside, and we feel indescribable and undeniable freedom in our healing.

Think of it this way: When you go to the doctor for a cough, the doctor looks for something deeper than your symptoms. He listens to your cough but looks further, knowing that there is a root issue causing it. He looks into your mouth, down into your throat, and sometimes even checks your lungs.

On this sixth step, we have made ourselves vulnerable and allowed God to help us find the reasons for our poor behavior and choices. He resolves the bad feelings we have by exposing and removing whatever caused them. As we trust Him for healing, the symptoms or unhealthy behaviors disappear.

When I arrived at this point, I was off medication and alcohol. My feelings of depression and anxiety had resolved, so there was no more need for prescriptions. My shopping craving was over, but my marriage still had some hitches in it. That made me feel trapped and angry. I surrendered these areas to God and began stepping through each of the levels again in an effort to peel back and expose both the cycles and roots of my pain.

Many times, we eliminate our addictions, eating disorders, harmful decisions, marriages, unhealthy relationships, and idolatry but hold on to fear, guilt, bitterness, depression, and anger. We wonder why we still feel rotten even though we are acting right. The trouble is that we still have some problems and are still sick. We are still giving satan legal ground; therefore, we are still in bondage.

This is the point at which we must choose to let go, not only of the pain but also of the burden. Our awareness so far has been hope, faith, prayer, reading, and worshiping. Now, we will add rest to our worship. These two things seem like apt counterbalances to one another; they actually necessitate one another. We need God's presence to rest in Him. Usher Him in and rest in His arms. Worship Him in Spirit and in truth, knowing that God inhabits our praise.

Steps matter. We want it all at once, but we can only do it one step at a time. We must be careful that by the time a step is accomplished, we are not too exhausted. We can rest and should always rest in Him, yet we cannot stop. If we stop and give in or up, we stay sick. If we use our exhaustion or fear as an excuse not to do more, then we have stopped healing. The resting I am talking about is getting into His presence to receive from His Spirit what you need to continue the journey. It is quiet time alone, allowing God to move in you.

The Lord Himself took time to rest from His labors (Genesis 2:2). He rested on the seventh day and still calls us to rest on the Sabbath. He asks us to take a break once a week, so rest must be important. The journey you are on is hard work. Not only do we need rest to gain strength for the next step, but often, we also need an interval of time while we process and understand more fully what He has done.

God is concerned for our well-being and promises to be our rest:

Come to Me, all you who are weary and burdened, and I will give you rest. Take My yoke upon you and learn from Me, for I am gentle and humble in heart, and you will find rest for your souls. For My yoke is easy and My burden is light.

Matthew 11:28–30 (NIV)

When we are in between the stairs, we are typically in one of two states: walking out the healing or taking God-ordained rest. The rest is when He fills us and readies us for the next challenge; it is mainly spiritual. Paul tells us of His travels to the third level in heaven as an example of resting in Him (2 Corinthians 12:2).

Rest does not always mean sitting in a lounge chair and sipping a fruity beverage. The rest we are discussing here is a kind of soaking submission to God. It is letting go of our thoughts, actions, schedules, ways, habits—everything—up to Him as we trust Him to move us in the direction we need to go.

Being still and silent when you want to scream and run is an example of soaking unto sanctification. It means relishing His renewing and refreshing.

While respite is a beautiful truth, it is also difficult to find. When Adam and Eve listened to the wrong voice and disobeyed God, the consequences marred our lives. In our fleshly state, it is hard to take proper rest in God. We seem to either be workaholics or TV-holics.

Yet the psalmist assures us that God has provided it: "The Lord is my shepherd; I have all that I need. He lets me rest in green meadows; He leads me beside peaceful streams" (Psalm 23:1–2, NLT).

Rest is a delicately designed, vulnerable state that requires great faith to enter. The rest demands we trust completely. It usually goes against everything we think or feel or want to do. Adherence to the state of rest seems to run opposite of our will.

Scripture explains that not to rest is to be disobedient:

> *There remains therefore a rest for the people of God. For he who has entered His rest has himself also ceased from his works as God did from His. Let us therefore be diligent to enter that rest, lest anyone fall according to the same example of disobedience. For the word of God is living and powerful, and sharper than any two-edged sword, piercing even to the division of soul and spirit, and of joints and marrow, and is a discerner of the thoughts and intents of the heart.*
>
> Hebrews 4:8–12 (NKJV)

Let us be diligent to enter His rest, lest we fall.

Only God Can Untangle It

Resting is good, especially before we begin to excavate roots out of our lives. Roots are the epicenter of our pain. They are the festering source from which the pain began. A root is born from a life hurt; we saw, felt, heard, tasted, or touched something that wounded us deep down. Some hurts are hard to face, but God will always cushion us and carry us to victory.

We need to relax and let the Lord gently lead us back to that place of pain so we can be healed. Going back there helps us to see whether or not the sting was our fault. Either way, we can then strip it of its control over our lives. Once God heals it, the issue is over, never to return. As the prophet said, "Forget the former things; do not dwell on the past. See, I am doing a new thing!" (Isaiah 43:18–19, NIV)

Sometimes, we may not remember the action or event that precipitated the painful issue. We may have blocked the starting place and do not even know where to look. God's Spirit can find any hidden pain and release our hurt. He will get to the pain, and we will allow Him to plant new roots in place of the old ones—roots of self-worth, security, love, peace, health, and a sound mind.

Many of my roots developed as an only child of divorced parents, many from an abusive marriage. My parents rarely disciplined me. I liked this plan. It suited me well until I realized that the rest of society was not on board with it. I went from delusions of grandeur right into being Queen of the Maskquerade. I was also free of abuse and then went right back to it, and here you can see that our healing takes time, and patience with yourself is pinnacle. Both were very abrupt and brutal transitions. Have you experienced being a victim to your upbringing or choices?

Even if our pain originated from somebody else's transgression, we have to choose to get out and get healed. We also have to admit we chose the wrong path. I dug deep with God to get out. I was determined to find the catalyst that activated my pain so that I could step back and let God remove it. To have played the victim would have put me right back into the devil's hands; I am convinced that he can destroy someone simply through the victim mentality, a tough mask to remove.

I had collected several roots and buried them deep down in tightly packed soil. The evil shoots began to intertwine and twist into a tangled ball. Roots like insecurity formed inside me due to a lack of biblical foundation, family instability, disobedience (from lack of discipline), rejection (from the divorces and my father's departure from the home), perfectionism (from performance mentality and the absence of foundation in Christ), sadness and co-dependency (from a lack of acceptance to leave the abuse for good), and fear (from a lack of belief, wisdom, and knowledge).

To make matters worse, I hardened my heart and covered it really well with a hopeless, controlling, stubborn disposition and a heaping dose of denial.

Stop, Look, and Listen

This step is difficult. We have to go as deep as we can for now, and we may shed many tears as we shed the pain. We will also realize many times that the pain was caused by something we were not even aware of. Sometimes, we need godly counsel and intervention through Christian counseling, another form of deeper guidance. We may need someone in front of us to wipe the tears away. God sends saints to stand alongside us—people who can look at us and connect to us spiritually during our healing (Romans 1:11; Acts 19:6).

If you feel as though you are going through your journey alone, make sure you are not alienating yourself or staying in false comfort out of fear. God gives abundantly if we remain in Him. When God directs a saint to enter your life, you will know their presence is divine and precious. Looking back on the company He sent into my own life, I can see how amazing and instrumental they were.

What I have learned is this: If something or someone hurts you, pay attention to it. Deal with it head-on in prayer. Remember that, no matter who hurt you, God is bigger than they are, and vengeance is His (Romans 12:19). He will protect and comfort you through changes you thought you could barely breathe through. I thought I was never, and I mean never going to break free from my now ex-husband, but with God, I did!

Follow God's "Program"

As different roots were exposed in my life, I asked forgiveness for my part. I repented for not trusting God sooner, and I obediently walked out on the next leg of healing, even if it meant not being able to see the next step. Whatever bad behaviors resulted from those roots, they vanished over time and with obedience. I do not know where they went, but they are undeniably forever gone.

The emotional stress in my life was subsiding, but I still suffered with some strongholds. There was a moment in which I had an epiphany; I realized that stepping up the heavenly staircase was a lifelong process. We want it all at once, all now. Accepting this fact was like accepting the fact that I was evil, and they both are key!

That does not mean we should tolerate strongholds. They are demonic, and you need to let God remove them. They are the negative areas in your life that seem to be chronic, as though they were glued to you. Hear this: they are not stuck to you, and you are not trapped. You have, however, allowed them to reign. You have ceded to the devil some legal ground in your soul. He is opportunistic and operates from that patch of territory.

When we know God is willing to recapture that ground for us, yet we refuse Him the room to operate in our lives, we are allowing the pain to reside in us. Do you see knots or tangles in your pain and healing? Where are they? Some areas clean out more easily than others. The devil has caulked in and duct-taped over the resistant ones. This is because you keep trying to fix the tangle. What you need to know is this: trust God, and He can undo the tangle.

I want us to see that not all the roots can come out at once. While some may be released, we need to be aware there may be more left in place. If we are obedient, God will remove all of them in His perfect timing. We need to have hope and faith for complete healing. We also embrace the reality of this being a process, a beautifully planned one. Our garden may not always be weed-free, but it will be glorious and fruitful as long as we are stepping in tune with the Father.

In my case, the wedding involved getting to a powerful root: fear. I had a great deal of frustration from my first marriage and a lot of fear that had formed a tangled knot that felt like it had paralyzed me deep in my soul. Terror became a learned response to not being able to let go and leave. I kept believing the lies he sped at me. It was an unhelpful response that cycled through the years of my life.

Just as falling while going down the stairs lands you at the bottom, running up the stairs usually involves skipping one or more of them. That was a revelation for me, one I am still trying to master. So many times, God extends His hand to me so that I can step back down and complete a step I raced past in my fury for the finish line.

He demands rest from us during this step. I felt like I was in slow motion on this stair. God had taken His hand and stopped me in my tracks. I was trying to outrun Him. I thought that if I just kept trucking, the pain would eventually disappear. Unfortunately, the pain was trucking right alongside me.

When I relented to believe He would provide if I stopped, God taught me true rest. He did this so I could see every move; each bend in my healing needed to be considered. He wanted me to be meticulous and allow Him to identify all of the roots so that I could resume my upward journey. He loved me enough to slow me down and clean me out again. It was uncomfortable. I felt vulnerable; the rest seemed odd.

What I failed to realize is that when we are sick, we are so far behind God that getting ahead of Him is not an option. Ironically, getting ahead of Him is just as defeating as living in the chariot's dust. Promotion without God's endorsement is not a promotion at all. In our newfound freedom, we need to be extremely careful not to strive for achievements that are outside of God's purpose.

Stepping into healing is hard; postponing what we think is progress is just as hard because we see it as a denial of our vision. We must rest in Him and allow His lead, His unction, His progress in us, and His timing. We must abandon the versions of progress that we generate from our limited thought capacity.

His version will undo the tangle, dismantle the ball, and then remove the roots slowly and steadily. When we get ahead of Him, we tend to run forward while dragging old roots and cycles with us. He calls us back because He knows we cannot take this baggage to the next level.

So, many times, we are afraid of the very thing that actually works because we cannot control it, explain it, or did not grow up with it. My passion for counseling comes from my life pains, and I definitely did not grow up with deliverance ministry, but it was exactly what I needed. It also taught me that helping others to do the same would help bring others closer to Christ.

Close the Gate

Christian counseling showed me how the lack of security growing up in a broken home and the breach of stability had weakened my faith. I wept for the loss I had experienced at such a young age. This also kept me fearful my children would experience the same, so I stayed in my first marriage way too long out of what? Fear! Why was I not worthy to have security, a good husband, a healthy family, and a safe place for me and my children? For all those years, I had let other people's faulty decisions determine my worth.

These types of issues become embedded in the family because no one closes the gate on them. Generational pain is anything ungodly that a parent, blood relative, or grandparent passes on to future generations. What losses have you endured from generational sins or curses? Which of these surprised you when God revealed them? How are you forgiving and moving past them? Have you let God remove the iniquity and close the gate?

Grief over losses we have neglected to face is an important part of our journey. We need to make sure we do not just react to the removal of the roots. We need to give ourselves time to rest and grieve the events and their effects. We need to allow God to help us to forgive and forget. We can allow the process to be sad. Matthew 5:4 (NIV) says, "Blessed are those who mourn, for they will be comforted."

Our goal is to acknowledge and release the root in order that it no longer continues to manifest. We will allow God to comfort us, and we will agree that it is okay to rest and lament. We will let the emotions run their God-ordained course: not too long, not too short, not too high, or too low if you know what I mean.

Ultimately, the grieving needs to stop; acceptance and forgiveness need to engulf the grief. What I did was to go backwards then forwards throughout my childhood and all the way through my young adult years—even through the hallways of my problem marriage and addictions.

The Spirit walked with me through healing. He took me to where the pain originated for that particular issue. He wiped my tears and helped to remove the roots, causing the pain, hurt, and sadness. He then removed guilt, fear, and unbelief for that specific issue. Then He told me to forgive.

Forgiveness is a critical part of healing. Until forgiveness is given and received, the root remains. Forgiveness is a multilevel tapestry and a difficult concept for us to understand. We need to allow God to help us along the path of forgiveness so that we know it is sincere and fruitful. True godly forgiveness is committing within your heart to forever forgo an offense and letting God remove the emotions attached.

Let go of what you can and only by God's direction. Release the shallow roots and the deep ones, too, if possible. Then fill yourself with God's love, His Spirit, and all of Isaiah 11:1–3. Stay far from entertaining them ever again. Be sensitive to allow the Spirit to walk with you back into your life to clean house, but never forget to fill it back up.

Luke 11:24–26 warns:

When an evil spirit comes out of a man, it goes through arid places seeking rest and does not find it. Then it says, 'I will return to the house I left.' When it arrives, it finds the house swept clean and put in order. Then it goes and takes seven other spirits more wicked than itself, and they go in and live there. And the final condition of that man is worse than the first.

Luke 11:24–26 (NIV)

Isaiah 11:1–3 counterattacks:

A shoot will come up from the stump of Jesse; from his roots a Branch will bear fruit. The Spirit of the LORD will rest on him – the Spirit of wisdom and of understanding, the Spirit of counsel and of power, the Spirit of knowledge and of the fear of the LORD – and he will delight in the fear of the LORD. He will not judge by what he sees with his eyes, or decide by what he hears with his ears;

Isaiah 11:1–3 (NIV)

A word to the wise: the step we are on can take hours, years, maybe decades. We need not rush it or get discouraged. God's great authority covers us. He has firmly planted us on His foundation. His ground is still, sound, powerful, without cracks, and never shifting or shaking. In this place of security, we can go back and relinquish any insecurity we have received from our earthly or extended family. The pain was and is no more. God has grafted us into a much bigger family.

Resist Generational Fallout

There is a lot of truth to generational curses and sin, but not in the sour grapes, blame-everybody-else kind of way. God even rebukes them in Ezekiel 18 for that mess. We need to break curses, but we also have to take up authority and responsibility to not receive or walk in them. God places the sins of our fathers not in our hearts but in our laps. When we grab hold, the habit activates, and pain takes root in the soul.

Unless they are broken by us, generational curses can function in the lives of people who are affected linearly simply by being born into the family. They literally fall into our laps, and in our weakness or ignorance, we pick them up according to Jeremiah 32:17–19:

Ah, Sovereign LORD, You have made the heavens and the earth by Your great power and outstretched arm. Nothing is too hard for You. You show love to thousands but bring the punishment for the fathers' sins into the laps of their children after them. O great and powerful God, whose name is the LORD Almighty, great are Your purposes and mighty are Your deeds, Your eyes are open to all the ways of men; You reward everyone according to his conduct and as his deeds deserve.

Jeremiah 32:17–19

We are not defenseless, even where generational sin is concerned. The choice is ours: we can carry the curse forward or stand against it and walk away free. If your family raised you in alcoholism, you are more likely to pick up the sin and take it with you. But, through prayer, worship, and rest in God, you can arrest the progress of the curse. Do you see yourself repeating the sins of your parents?

Maybe we are not standing bellies up to the bar these days, but our bellies might still be parked in the back pew trying to cop a read of someone else's highlighted Bible in judgment. How does this affect our spiritual health differently than drinking does?

The Maskquerade Palace

My mother obviously did not think my stepdad was as much fun as I thought he was, so she left him. After they divorced, we moved out of the big family home in the suburbs and into a condominium that sat just behind a gas station flanking the highway surrounding the city. From my teen years up into my very early twenties, I lived in the "roach" room atop the condominium's castle tower. It is here that the future title, Queen of the Maskquerade, was formed.

My foundation had crumbled, and satan routinely nudged me. Every choice we make, whether we realize it or not, is a choice for God or for the devil. Each decision builds on the foundation of promise or failure. There are no neutral choices. A biblical example: read the account of Laodicea in Revelation 3:14–22. When God infills us with His Holy Spirit and removes the roots of our pain, we are able to choose success over failure.

The weakness of the flesh is well documented throughout Scripture. Paul describes it powerfully:

> *I know that nothing good lives in me, that is, in my sinful nature. For I have the desire to do what is good, but I cannot carry it out. For what I do is not the good I want to do; no, the evil I do not want to do—this I keep on doing.*

> Romans 7:18–19 (NLT)

Left unchecked, the weakness of the flesh feeds the roots of our pain. As you look back and walk through your life story, you will notice where each root issue began. You will see which roots have been addressed and which have been suppressed. You will be able to identify the stream of pain in your life. For me, much of the pain trafficked through insecurity and disobedience.

Living in a condominium with a single mother and very little discipline, I developed an unwarranted independence and defiance to authority. My mother provided as best she could but was physically incapable of filling the role of the complete family unit I so craved. This lack birthed and nurtured bad roots in my life.

We lived on the outskirts of an affluent area. The kind of town where you carried the expensive purses and drove the shiniest cars, both smelling of true cowhide. I attended school in this well-heeled (but unfortunately, not necessarily healed) part of Atlanta. Eighth-graders attended the local high school. I was among the class of sub-freshman when we arrived.

As I mentioned earlier, we were not even a football field away from the Baptist Church that buffered us from the onslaught of interstate traffic Atlanta would produce hourly. It was not just a church but a mega church. It was like having an enormous, flashing billboard in our yard that screamed, "Go to church, you fools. I have put one right next to your mailbox!"

God could not have made it more obvious. Yet, we never went, not even once.

The cool kids at this new high school accepted me. That spoke volumes; they were rich, spoiled, and had cliques dating back to their Pre-K Days, and my purses smelled of plastic (there is a sad irony in that statement). They did not take well to newcomers. Satan made sure I fit in with popular group; I made cheerleading and got so mixed up with the social order that I neglected to study and read. Take note of where satan has set you up for a fall. And know this: your purpose is often found in the very things the devil convinces you are purposeless.

The roots of appearance, idolatry, and social structure began to grow in me during this time. I allowed my identity to be based in what others thought of me. That root began to birth disappointment, jealousy, bitterness, perfectionism, and more insecurity. I had very little self-worth beyond their glowing opinions of me. As we have clearly seen, our identity is to be based in Christ.

There is healing in knowing that God did not intend for us to covet or compete with one another. This is so important that He mentioned it in His top-ten list of principles (Exodus. 20:17) and wrote it in stone twice.

During my stint in high school, I left the track team. Track was an area in which my abilities were strong. This gifting could have eventually paid for my college tuition. I ran a five-six-minute mile with little effort and carried a 4.0 average. In fact, the high school coach in our old district had already integrated me into his team when I was in sixth grade.

When we moved to the condo, I replaced running with cheerleading. Boys and status replaced my studies; the world order replaced my childhood innocence. Society became my backbone. Evil seeds began to take root. I no longer ran, and my grades were at best Cs and Ds.

Look back and dig deep to find the talents you had as a young child. Remember the purpose God has for you. He never changes, and His purposes never change; we just hinder them. The pain and hurt hide the promise and purpose. This concealment becomes an unhealthy protection mechanism.

My mom had that condominium, the one behind the church we never attended, decked to the hilt. She maxed every credit card to make the place and me look beautiful. I began to manifest a root that would sprout divorce, bankruptcy, eating disorders, severe depression and anxiety, and addiction.

Notice that I said that I looked beautiful. I did not feel beautiful. Roots of idolatry, covetousness, and greed can make us poor, not just financially but spiritually and emotionally. Thankfully, my future deliverance will make me the proud recipient of God-ordained prosperity. He is not bound by earthly cash-driven commerce, which is our ignorance and, sadly, our security. Many times, it's fleeting. The devil wants us to live in financial defeat, but the Lord wants us to live in abundance. (For more on this kind of prosperity, Malachi 3:10.)

By its very nature, godly prosperity is indescribable. God's profusion encompasses things like joy, peace, purity, truth, wisdom, health, and fruitfulness. I find it difficult to formulate words that are multifaceted enough to describe these miracles. I want to make sure that we do not misunderstand prosperity by placing it in an earthly context that is limited to material possessions.

Right next to my bedroom in the condominium, there was a tanning bed installed. I remember seeing the faint glow of purple oozing out from under the attic door daily. The tanning salon attic was where the roaches lived while we were awake. We weren't the only residents of the condo; we shared it with a colony of roaches. These were physical roaches, but looking back, I realize there were many more on a spiritual level.

I would wake up in the middle of the night, knowing the bugs would scatter as soon as I turned on the light. The sight is enough to send you reeling. Roach movements are not predictable; they are fast and devious and have the ability to circumvent obstacles by sliding through tiny cracks.

To this day, I have an aversion to these things. They say for every one you see, there are countless numbers in the walls and surrounding land. What a nasty thought—and another truth for Demon Training 101. Demons reflect the same behavior. Light makes them scatter; just because you cannot see them does not mean they are not in attendance.

One time, ticks covered the stairs leading up to my room. There were twenty or thirty of them, and they were all alive. I had to pick them up one at a time and flush them. Unlike the roaches, which are merely filthy and carry disease, these guys are parasitic, and they feed off blood. Blood sucking is not a life-giving characteristic.

I learned at a young age that if anything was going to get done, I had best do it myself. When it comes to healing, we need not look around for someone else to initiate. Healing with God and godly guidance is the surest and best way. God sends others to help, but we hold no expectation of our offenders sharing in the workload. Root issues are our issues, even if someone else caused them. If we wait for our perpetrators to release a root by apologizing to us, we postpone our healing.

The roaches had to be removed, and I had to do it myself (for decades, sadly enough). I scraped together some change and got as many roach motels as I could afford. I remember they smelled like dog food when you had sixteen of them together. I lined them up like soldiers, side by side in a row. They formed a protective barrier between my bed and the attic door.

Not only did they block out some of the purple glow, they allowed me to feel a little better about going to bed at night. The funny thing is that when we try to solve things ourselves, our solutions rarely have any effect on the actual problem. The roach motels trapped lots of roaches but never eliminated the source of the infestation. The solution we conjure is awareness; it affords temporary peace and subdues our negative feelings.

I should have also put a wet towel under the other door to stop the smoke from coming in from my mother's incessant puffing downstairs. It would not have helped for long; I soon picked the smoking curse off my lap and gave it place in my life. I was the only fifteen-year-old, cigarette-smoking cheerleader with my own ashtray.

The smoke was not all that smelled at our house. We had an undisciplined dog as well; imagine that. He had some major root issues. The dog that bit my mother's lip clear off was as undisciplined as I was. He was a tick magnet, too, and he liked the roaches. He would actually eat them.

He was a beautiful buff-colored cocker spaniel named Buffington, Buffy for short. This dog used the dining room table and chairs as a restroom, saturating the carpet with urine below every chair and table leg. We could not afford a new carpet, but the smell got so bad that after years of urine, I finally convinced Mom of an alternate solution. I would pull up the soiled area of the carpet, clean whatever was underneath, and cover it with a floor rug. She agreed.

How often do we use this method to try to heal? We try to cut away the broken parts and fill them in with something that looks better. Yet, the problem remains unsolved. That was how life went in the Maskquerade Palace. The cover-up and partial removal methods do not extract the root of the issue or solve the real problem.

Divine Solutions Are the Answer

Our condo story perfectly illustrates my point: Parasites and disease-carrying insects infested the house, yet no exterminator was called. Our dining room smelled of urine and was full of toxic smoke; we just lived with it. The attic contained a nuclear, neon light bed that addressed no legitimate need (and we had many). We had a vicious animal and tons of alcohol in the house; nothing changed. Strange men slipped in and out, but no father sat in the big chair where the remote control lay. There were drawers full of revealing clothes and even drugs; there were no church visits scheduled on our calendar full of shopping sprees. Now, how many bad seeds were planted in our lives? Yet nothing of benefit or true value was allowed in. No rest for the weary there.

Our next steps are so necessary for the endurance of our healed state. They will begin to add into the empty places left from the removal of all the pain. Obedience is a step God can bless abundantly. Pick your chin up, look around, and start looking for blessings as you tread through this next chapter. It is the area is where my deepest passion lies; it is also the place where so many people give up.

Please keep stepping upward, my beautiful, mask-removing friend. We are entering territory that will cement our healing. The next two chapters form a mini-transition; we empty out to fill up, and learn how to "sew into" God.

Are you staying in the Word and walking it out as James 1:22 tells us to do? The pastor cannot do it for you. You must step out in the truth of God's Word. You may not have stepped perfectly all the time, but you are coming to a place of adherence. Don't quit!

It is amazing when we look back from a healed and healing perspective. We begin to see where God ordained hope and where we finally chose Him. We see where we allowed Him to replace the old root with the root of the Word through faith-filled rest in Him (Ephesians 3:17–21; Colossians 2:6–7).

This takes us up to our next step: obedience. It will ensure our healing and keep the pain away. Authority, accountability, discipline, obedience—these are all words people want to run from or falsely own. In reality, authentically achieved, they are steps toward freedom. They are actions we need to take if we want to be healed.

Congratulations! You have released many bad roots unto God. You have also added a new awareness! You are resting in His arms. Do not grow weary in well doing for this process.

Chapter Seven

OBEDIENT AS A PALACE GUARD

Step Seven: Step Into Obedience Through Fasting

"Whatever you have learned or received or heard from me or seen in me—put it into practice. And the God of peace will be with you"

(Philippians 4:9, NIV)

Many women struggle with obedience. They are overwhelmed and believe that finding a quiet moment to do God's bidding is impossible.

Obedience often feels like the fragment of a coal in your running shoe of life. It irritates your foot all the way to the bubble bath of peace. You see it as an obstacle and want to remove it. In truth, it will become a diamond of provision if you will leave it in place and subject it to the pressure of your endurance (2 Corinthians 12:7–10).

We will learn ways to embrace this step forever—and with joy. While we always need to allow Him to deal with our issues, we are now adding good habits and godly actions to support our endurance. Our healing and purpose depend on our fortitude in sticking with God's ways indefinitely.

God's expectations are clear in the Old Testament. He called them His law and then exemplified them perfectly in His Son. So often, we excuse one another from obedience by casually saying we are in the dispensation of grace. While God has saved us by grace (everyone would be on a hot road to hell if He hadn't), we are not exempt from His decrees, if we want power and blessing.

We are exempt from attaining salvation by adherence to rules, but it is not an excuse for sin. Paul challenges the implications of free will by asking, "What shall we say, then? Shall we go on sinning so that grace may increase? By no means! We died to sin; how can we live in it any longer?" (Romans 6:1–2, NIV)

God's rules in the New Testament are love, faith, brotherly love, the fruit, the Great Commission, evangelism, sanctification, praise, worship, prayer, fasting, giving, listening, resting, and turning from evil, among others. We will attain to them if we crucify our flesh and allow Him to give us His Spirit.

Christ came to fulfill the law, which He did. He did not abolish God's edicts. If you look closely at the behavior of those who are being sanctified by His Spirit, their conduct reflects adherence to none other than His law!

In the garden, God's only requirement from Adam was that he not eat from one tree. With all the lures and ungodly options surrounding us today, I would love a simple list of commandments that said:

1. Do not eat from the tree in the middle of your front yard.

2. End of stone tablet.

Every inclination of our hearts is toward evil. To me, that means pain. God tells us this in the first book of the Bible (see Genesis 6:5). I think He wanted to make sure we did not start out in denial. He reiterates our deficiency of holiness often. We are sinful and need not only a page of commandments but also a book full of pages of commandments.

I realize that God commands us to love. That does not mean that you rip your Bible in two and commence a grace period. In Matthew 22:37–40 (NIV), Jesus said, "Love the Lord your God with all your heart and with all your soul and with all your mind." This is the first and greatest commandment. And the second is like it: "Love your neighbor as yourself."

All the law and the prophets hang on these two commandments. This book cumulates in His love; to know the depths of His love, we must assume His Son's likeness into the very fabric of our actions. One big blaring point to add to this is the obvious fact that we cannot love like Him unless we simply let Him love us first. Please let Him love you!

The law consists of the entire Bible, precept upon precept, without excuse or exception. I am not advising strict regulation to a law that Christ fulfilled. Habitual nonsense is unnecessary and is a good way for satan to keep us busy. I am pointing to the respect that is due every word of God; I am talking about our accountability in allowing the Spirit to impose God's ways and Word on our lives and even our trials.

Proverbs 30:5 (NIV) stresses the perfection of God's Word: "Every word of God is flawless; He is a shield to those who take refuge in Him."

His commandments should be kept. While this is impossible in our flesh, it is possible with our Spiritual infilling of His Holy Spirit. I am not talking about all Levitical law. I am talking about forgiveness, mercy, grace, love for our enemies, communion, prayer, fasting, giving, and consuming His Word—anything and everything that pleases Him.

I even feel a pull to honor His feasts Leviticus 23:1–2. He says to keep them! The apostles and Jesus kept them, so why not us? We need to be on His calendar all the time. We ignore precious commands because we were never taught or are unwilling to undo our mindset. Lord, let us have the mind of Christ!

We live in grace, and we obey through grace. Grace is the only way to true healing, but we must reside in that grace in due course by obeying His decrees. We allow His glory to pass through us to refine us to obey continually.

You could hear the crickets chirping as I sat alone night after night, day after day, hour after hour, week after week, immersed in God's Word. I would stop only to sleep. God's isolation will teach us how imperative discipline is to our success and well-being.

In my isolation from the world, I was not displacing addiction. I was captivated by God's love. This time, I was not trying to fill a void. God was packing in what He needed me to have for my healing to stick.

There were so many empty places left by the removal of what the world had planted in me. My Vicki D. would always say, "When you feel them, the empty spots, drink in the Spirit like water and feel it running in, filling up all the areas left open."

We will succeed, not by our might but by His Spirit (see Zechariah 4:6). Once again we reference Zechariah because here, discipline unto obedience becomes tolerable and accomplishable.

The Fast Track to Adherence

Now, we will add fasting to our list of awareness. God calls us to difficult tasks and one of the hardest things to do is to stop eating. Nourishment sustains life, and most of us enjoy not just eating but gorging ourselves at times.

We can read the first chapter of Daniel as one of many good references to fasting. God gave Daniel, Shadrach, Meshach, and Abednego knowledge, wisdom, and insight because of their obedience to fasting (Daniel 1:17).

We will ask Him for the things that matter to Him during our fast. Solomon just asked Him for His wisdom. He gave Solomon so much more because he asked for only what mattered to God.

He has already healed us and is healing us daily. We have the record of accomplishment to support our faith for the next request. God does not suggest that we give, pray, and fast. He tells us to do these things, saying, "When you give," "When you pray," and "When you fast" (Matthew 6:2, 5, 16).

When we fast, we do so healthfully and with professional advice, if necessary. (Seek your doctor's input, particularly if you have any health issues.) We seek God for His timing and process. We then commence prayer to get us through. We commit, start, and do not cheat or stop until our intended conclusion.

We fast for Christ, not for blessing. We fast because He gave us the knowledge of His expectation of this promise. If you fast with a pure heart, you will experience a peace that is inexplicable and worth the trial. He even tells us in His Word that some issues can only be resolved through fasting (Mark 9:29).

I remember once, I had just come off a three-day fast and was heating up wax to use for a project. I remember putting the wax in the microwave for a minute longer than usual. When I pulled it out, the steam was so aromatic I had to take it outside.

I was in a hurry and waited a moment for the steam to exhaust itself outdoors. Then I went back inside and began to work. When I finished, I closed the jar and realized that steam was still pouring out of the sides of the closed lid. I did not want to cause the jar to expand and break, so I decided to remove the cap. When I did, the jar tilted and slipped. The hot wax covered my hand. It looked like I was trying to cast a mold of my hand. The coverage of wax was thick and consistent.

I heard a sizzle and hiss as my skin became singed under the thick, waxy coating. The layer was stuck to me like glue. The burn and piercing sting began to travel up my fingers, hand, and arm. It was excruciating. My mind raced as I thought about a relative who had been in the hospital days earlier from a similar burn incident.

Quickly, my thoughts went to faith. My mouth opened and professed with belief for healing, "Jesus, heal my skin." God instantaneously healed me.

Now, I still had to withstand the hours it took to remove half a jar of drying, sticky wax off my hand, arm, floor, and countertop. My fingers were the size of cucumbers, but there was no pain, no burnt skin, nothing. Because of my obedience to His ways and His Word, I knew exactly what to do. He heals through grace and mercy with His love and our faith.

You have been methodically collecting life applications, too. You have learned to practice hope, faith, prayer, reading, worship, and rest. Now, you are ready for fasting.

In this step, there are three devices that lead us into obedience, and there are three warnings. Past steps have been hard but in a different way. They were steps out of sickness and into healing; they were vulnerable and raw. Now that we have a little more strength, the next two stairs form a transition; while needed for our healing, they also begin to push us toward staying healed.

Marching up the Stair of Obedience

We have seen from our stepping so far that we can only obey through grace. Our own righteousness goes before Him as filthy rags (Isaiah 64:6); His righteousness empowers us (1 Corinthians 1:30).

Between growing up with a military father and having an all-or-nothing personality, obedience is akin to breathing for me. In fact, this important truth is the very heart of this book. I have already told you that I am most passionate about this step. When we are passionate, we tend to have trouble conveying simple methods to those who see the topic or practice as unappealing or difficult. Knowing this, I called my mentor and asked her for help. Many times, when I cannot see things, she can help me understand and see things better.

I asked her to explain to me how she would describe victorious obedience. She told me that in her Spirit, she saw three components to proper compliance: see, receive, and act. Her words literally turned the switch for me. I had been acting without needing to know why. When she articulated this concept, her terminology became the mini-steps I needed to convey.

Immediately, I prayed that God would show me this in His Word. He took me to Philippians 4:9 (NIV): "Whatever you have learned or received or heard from me, or seen in me—put it into practice. And the God of peace will be with you."

When we just see or hear, we are still in operation mode and not yet what I call flow mode. We must do what we have seen or heard, even if it is difficult. Now, our hearing is where the activation of the Word resides (Romans 10:17). It becomes two actions in one: seeing and then the activation that comes through hearing. Activation is when the Word comes alive in you and leads you into a changed behavior—the sign of reception and true learning.

The second mini-step is to receive and learn through the activation. This also involves two actions in one. We must receive first in order to learn. The Holy Spirit commences our understanding, which lies within our hearts. As we learn to crucify our flesh, it becomes natural to reside in the Spirit and obey. Then comes the third mini-step, doing or acting on what we know is true regardless of what we feel.

Job's righteousness was in direct relation to his obedience. My obedience to leaving my first marriage, sobriety, and discipline have made it easier to walk in faith. My obedience to leaving the abuse of my first marriage has blessed me beyond measure. My obedience to overcome fear and walk in faith has helped me to master my faith, which is the vessel for healing.

Your obedience is determining your path of healing right now.

Detoxification from the Poison of Emptiness

When pain is the central feature of our lives, we are toxic, spiritually and often physically. I have seen this in my own life.

Several of the first nights during my (thirty-three-year-old) detox, I had to get up, peel off my pajamas, and change the sheets. There was a splash of water that hit the floor as I wrung out my hair; it unnerved me. I had sweat through the mattresses and my pajamas. The drugs had confused my entire system. I did not realize how sick they were making me until I allowed all the drugs to come out, and it took days. Watching the poison leave my natural body was bone-chilling, almost unbearable, and desperately sad.

I felt like I was going to self-destruct. I knew obedience had arrived, and I was unsure of how much I liked it, if at all. Have you felt the same disdain for adherence to your process? Can you see how your endurance has brought you out so far? How has your success added to your faith?

These were not the questions I immediately asked myself that morning. When we arrived at the hospital, they inquired as to my condition. I explained every detail and then waited patiently for a response.

"She could very easily have multiple seizures during this transition. You will have to make sure she does not swallow her tongue. If you plan to stay at home, you have a lot to think about."

The nurse, rather nonchalantly, told me the frightening news. Her tone was shocking, considering the weight of the information she was presenting.

Swallow my what? I thought I needed a pill to keep that from happening. I was serious; gagging on my tongue did not sound like healing to me.

Because of how long and how much of the drug I had been ingesting, the nurse wanted to place me in the hospital to detoxify safely. I will never forget sitting in the waiting room and being asked to enter the admission room. The seriousness of my toxicity was plain.

Unfortunately, getting the drugs out of our system is not as easy as putting them in; detoxification was, for me, hell on earth. From my perspective, if I had not endured this period of hell on earth, I would have endured the real hell for all eternity. The drugs were blocking the Spirit in my life. This concept God proved true when, after six months of sobriety, the Spirit finally entered in His fullness. He needs a clean, willing vessel.

When your prescription is fifteen years in the making, detox is just the beginning of the end. The next step was to babysit me every day, away from my children, in the circle of chairs room (outpatient rehab). God blessed me with the "out" part of outpatient; however, it required that I do the "up" part of stepping up. It was not easy. This step up is synonymous with obedience.

We looked for a facility that would work. We visited some of the nastiest places with some of the weirdest people in the world in attendance. I begged and pleaded; I did not need treatment. It went in one ear and out the other, and I went straight in the facility.

I quickly learned not to judge in my deceived state. I fit the description of a weirdo myself, and I was not going to let anyone enable me any longer. I had to be obedient to God and the process. Skipping steps was not going to cut it.

Not only was I undisciplined, but I was, as you know, "My mask of the Kingdom of Pain and Woe Is Me," the reigning wreck who was now on her way to stepping through the gate and into the court of doing. I was about to become a daughter of the Most High!

The far better place I was looking for was a way off yet. Psalm 84:2 (NIV) says, "My soul yearns, even faints, for the courts of the LORD." I yearned... and waited...and pressed.

God proved to me that our preparation, pressing, and positioning for healing are relative to how much or how little we allow God to work. Our obedience is inadequate without His Spirit, but His Spirit responds to our desiring Him above all else. "As the body without the spirit is dead, so faith without deeds is dead" (James 2:26, NIV). Works complete our faith and are a natural outgrowth of walking in faith. Works equal obedience by their very nature, yet still, they cannot occur outside of God's grace.

I consider discipline to be a work for and of God. As we account, we can see where He requires us to attempt to attain the impossible before the possible can divinely be imparted. Anything that takes crucifying our flesh unto God is unnatural to us. I surrendered with one eye closed, and my fists clenched tightly. I finally allowed God to decide what I was doing for the day. I determined to obey Him on the highest and most reputable level I could humanly attain. It was a new day and a new step; obedience had arrived.

Duty Delivers Us from Defiance

The Lord says in His Word that obedience is better than sacrifice.

But Samuel replied, "What is more pleasing to the LORD: your burnt offerings and sacrifices or your obedience to His voice? Listen! Obedience is better than sacrifice, and submission is better than offering the fat of rams"

(1 Samuel 15:22, NLT)

That is a powerful statement. He wants us to see and listen "to His voice." When we are fasting, we are able to better hear the voice of God. When you study Scripture, we learned in Chapter Two that it is our "hearing gate," where the Word enters, and thus faith grows. We all, as humans, have a threefold nature: Body, Soul, and Spirit. We also have five senses, essentially, five gates that enter our body and into our soul only one sense enters the Spirit: sight, smell, hearing, taste, and touch. Hearing enters into our Spirit.

The Old Testament tells about our need to bring sacrifices in order to commune with God. Jesus has fulfilled the sacrificial system. However, God did not dole out a list of rules merely to fill up a stone tablet. He did not do it just for the Old Testament folks. The law shows us our inability without His Spirit; the law teaches us about His ways, His preferences, and how he expects us to act (Galatians 3:24).

When Christ returned to heaven, and Pentecost rolled around—bam!—the infilling of His Spirit engraved His laws in men's hearts. As 2 Corinthians 3:3 (NIV) puts it: "You show that you are a letter from Christ, the result of our ministry, written not with ink but with the Spirit of the living God, not on tablets of stone but on tablets of human hearts."

While we are always struggling with our nasty ways, His ways come more naturally to us as we change into His likeness. The birthing point for the nine fruits of the Spirit (Galatians 5:22–26) is love, joy, peace, patience, kindness, goodness, faithfulness, gentleness, and one that we definitely need for obedience to take its full work—self-control. In order for a tree to produce fruit, its roots must be good and go deep. Let God plant good roots so we may produce fruit in keeping with repentance (Matthew 3:8 and 10).

Be patient (a fruit); do not let the devil deceive you into giving up. Tripping is normal. Half the time, I am looking down on each step, checking my shoelaces. Everybody stumbles along the way. Every once in a while, we need to return to a previous step because if we do not see the beginnings of a trend toward Christ's likeness, then we have missed a stair somewhere.

Keep doing your "duty." Do not get discouraged. If the trend seems to be going in reverse, pray and ask God to reveal the missing stair. He will show you which step you need to revisit. Obedience is not easy, but through your obedience, your faith grows.

Now, if healing is a staircase, the relationship is the handrail. When we trust and obey God, we begin to build a relationship with our Father. We step into the seeing and hearing deep within our Spirit that we desperately need. When the relationship deepens, the ability to adhere to the step becomes easier. We move from seeing and hearing and enter the place of receiving and learning.

Time is essential to maturity. Obedience is just like hope; at first, it feels manufactured, but as time and maturity develop, it becomes a part of our lives. The doing part starts to happen.

Three Slippery Steps

Before we continue, let me say this: While there are three steps to obedience, there are also three things, in my experience, that make compliance difficult: a lack of discipline, ignorance to society's wrong methods (displacement), and genuine fear (which is the opposite of faith).

Discipline is a very important part of healing. We have talked about it before in more practical terms. I am not talking now about ten miles on the treadmill every day. I am talking about love and genuine passion for wanting to please God. "Spare the rod and spoil the child" is true. The Shepherd has a rod for discipline, direction, guidance, and protection for His sheep. Keeping our healing takes discipline and obedience.

When I started writing *The Maskquerade*, I had to clear the pages of streams of unhealthy actions and thoughts that I was not ready to face yet, a perfect example of my denial of my sick marriage. The first edition, entitled *The Roach Princess,* was filled with masks that I did not even know I was wearing. I needed a lesson in continuing to progress and listening to God in order to obey regardless of fear.

My chronicle was lopsided because I was missing discipline to a plan, the glue that binds ideas together. This step allowed me to see and hear my pain, and it taught me how I healed. Upon accepting the need for this discipline, I knew I needed advice for the how-to of writing a book. A book takes diligence and is a labor of love.

Healing takes obedience, slowing down, listening to trusted authority, and digging deep. Healing is just the training camp for your true purpose in life. How excited are you about your purpose? Are you glad to know that all you have to do is obey God and you are in training for your mighty purpose?

My prior discipline (in walking out the steps described in this book) taught me how to implement them to complete this project. The successful experience of traveling the path was necessary for the doing that was required to complete the book. I felt incapable and wanted to give up. What I was capable of was seeing my lack, listening to good counsel, hearing the voice of God, receiving criticism, learning the necessary techniques, and then doing them. I got the input I needed, wrote the book, and, to be honest, it was just as hard as healing from divorce, fear, and rejection, only in a different way because it had to be revised to be right!

We have been through hell for a reason. Let us begin to switch our focus as we mount this step. We will be transformed as we receive and learn from seeing and hearing, and then we will turn it all into doing. We begin to start walking in our healed and healing state with power, knowing our abilities as we summon our divine purpose to come to the surface and compel us forward.

We can pray, read, fast, rest, listen, persevere, and, above all else, obey. Hebrews 10:16 (NIV) quotes the Holy Spirit: "This is the covenant I will make with them after that time, says the Lord. I will put My laws in their hearts, and I will write them on their minds."

Then He adds: "Their sins and lawless acts I will remember no more" (Hebrews 10:17, NIV). He makes us able. We receive the ability in our hearts and minds that enables us to do what we are called to do.

The three slick steps can catch you off guard. Be alert and examine your heart and life. What happens behind closed doors? How does your heart react to pain when no one is looking? We know that many of our problems are rooted in a lack of discipline. Where defiance reigns, ignorance and pain are flourishing. Uproot these lies and keep moving upward.

As always, God gives us a choice. Jeremiah 21:8 (NIV) says, "Furthermore, tell the people, 'This is what the LORD says: See I am setting before you the way of life and the way of death.'"

Obedience is a step consisting of multiple parts. Each mini-step can lead to life or death. Christ showed us discipline through His own humble love and obedience unto death. All of it is for our healing.

In our pain and sickness, the greatest culprit is our fear. My years of anxiety and panic disorder proved this fact. My biggest fear was fear; in point of truth, our biggest fear needs to be God.

The devil takes our weaknesses and trumps them. But God never intended us to fear. He intended for us to use feelings of anticipation, grounded by faith, to propel us into greatness. Find the opposite of your downfall, and there your blessing will be.

In my life, Christ makes parallels to show me what is going on in the heavenly realm. We are fleshly beings, and physical examples are very easy for us to grasp. I have mentioned how He used the house, the owl, and the divorce to show me in the physical realm what He was doing in the supernatural or spiritual in my life. When you are obedient to intercession, the natural will line up with God's intent for your life. He arranged it this way so that we would not miss Him because all His work is done in the Spirit first.

God has positioned me to minister His Word publicly. At one point, public speaking was tough for me. In our flesh, exposure makes most want to run back down the stairs. I cannot; my life is to serve Christ, so I serve in the capacity He intended. I walk the anticipation out in faith by His love.

"There is no fear in love; but perfect love casts out fear, because fear involves torment. But he who fears has not been made perfect in love" (1 John 4:18, NKJV).

He wants us to look fear in the face and remove our sword from its sheath without even contemplating the fears involved. This sword is the Word of God as described in Hebrews 4:12 and Ephesians 6:17. We are still journeying into the faith place; until we arrive in the heavenly Jerusalem, fear will come calling, but by walking in His perfect love, we will fear not.

My obedience to overcome fear on thrill rides paralleled His teaching me to overcome and rule out fear of all kinds when it came to Him. That drop-in-the-stomach feeling, onstage or off, is something I wanted to be done with; I wanted to place it in the past. This may seem silly to you. God's dealing with me through frightening physical experiences may seem trivial, but fear was the manifestation of my largest root and all the subsequent roots.

I decided to zip-line with a group in Mexico. When our guide, Pepe, led us out onto the suspended wire, I gulped. We had a mesh platform jutting from the mountainside 300 feet above the jungle floor and only a repel line straight down to lead us out. I grabbed Pepe's shirt and hollered, "Get the donkey! I'm riding back!"

Pepe grinned and led me to what I felt sure was my death. I never looked to Christ, and I failed him because, in my fear, I never looked to him for comfort. All he wanted to do was to tell me to look up during my jungle terror. All Pepe wanted to do was argue with me about Jesus having never ridden a burro. The lesson in this exercise is this: Dropping hundreds of feet without dying will kill at least part of your fear.

I prayed for months that God would forgive me and give me another chance to overcome fear and prove to God that I believed. God still had to heal that trust, and He did. Months later, I was standing atop a Mayan Pyramid water drop called "Leap of Faith." The devil taunted me. I froze in fear. I accepted the faulty information instead of casting it out and trusting the Holy Spirit, whom Christ gave me for protection and comfort.

I climbed all the stairs, praying, "God, thank You. I know this is Your will. Thank You for giving me a second chance."

I even saw the word believe tattooed on a woman's back at the top of the pyramid. I looked down. We were hundreds of feet above a shark pool. You had to leap off the side and fall hundreds of feet. The slide would then capture you and shoot you through the pool of sharks.

I froze. I took my eyes off the cross. I turned around and went back down the stairs. As horrible as it sounds, that is what I did. I took the wide path— you know, the one where if you stumble, you fall all the way down. I failed God in my fear. I repented and prayed, "Forgive me, and please give me one last chance, Father."

He did not even wait a month. "Jesus!" I whispered as I looked away from the dark tube I was about to enter. I switched my fearful focus to the bright, beautiful sky. My stomach ached. The acid churned as the adrenaline stirred it. My vision was off and on from the lack of oxygen. The tunnel was tight and dark all the way to the bottom. I thought how difficult it would be to breathe once I entered. The air was already dense and thick even at its opening.

"Jesus, without You, I am incapable, claustrophobic, and terrified. Help me, Lord. Calm me, I need Your strength. In my weakness, You are strong" (2 Corinthians 12:9).

I repeated a scripture as the fear arose in my throat. The tube was long and built into a mountainside. You could not even track the path prior to entering the buried passageway.

I sat at the pinnacle of a trinity of waterslides: "Nightfall," "Three Fall," and "Freefall." I sat there terrified. Fear is not an option in the Kingdom and God, however. He was making sure I trusted Him above all else.

I sat atop a mound of fear with not one challenge but three: one for each failure and one for good faith. I felt like Peter, who was faced with three opportunities to deny Jesus. Nevertheless, my plan was to conquer "Nightfall" and do the rest much later.

Silly as this may seem to you, falling off things horrified me. Every step that I climbed caused me pain. My muscles would lock up. I felt like I was progressing, but I was not moving forward. The higher stairs were the hardest. This elevation was where the faith line would become hard to find, and we would have to stop and rest. I would have to listen to the voices in my head. In the stillness, I would cast out the fearful ones and replace them with faith. This time, I knew not to take my eyes to Jesus. Every step closer tightened my chest and paralyzed my muscles.

Finally, I was at the top, and it was my turn. I gave in to my weak knees and sat down. "Oh Lord, this is dark, and I am scared; Holy Spirit, please comfort me!" I said as the lifeguard commanded that I go.

I did not even know where I was going, but I had faith. I crossed my legs and arms and pushed myself into the black abyss. The dark, tight tube embraced me with thick air that was hard to take in and let out.

I panicked and began to spiral into anxiety. The war zone was in my mind. I was battling between Christlike thoughts of relaxing and allowing the ride to carry me and thoughts of "I am stuck...bound...closed in...cannot breathe...cannot escape...cannot get out...trapped."

The air became fresh, cool, and palpable instantaneously as I hit the light. "Thank You, Jesus! Thank You for faith," I whispered.

I did not know how much my faith had grown. I hoped enough to conquer the remaining two rides. I decided for a moment to let it sink in before climbing again. I rested in God.

Again, I made my way up the stairs. Knowing my fate this time, I resided in Christ. I cast out bad thoughts and kept my eyes focused in the right direction. I made it through two of the three slides. I had "Freefall" left to conquer.

I had to ride through another dark tube for an undisclosed amount of time, which would eventually drop me hundreds of feet straight down into a pool. For the third time, I sat there looking into the pitch-black unknown. I looked to my right as my fear began to well up and saw the word believe on a girl's headband. The word was no less beautiful than a crown of Awareness upon her head. At that instant. My flesh was crucified, and my Spirit and I finally took the "Leap of Faith!"

I leaped in faith.

The slide was dark. The incline steepened. I used my last breath to pronounce, "Jesus!" I bellowed His name as my stomach muscles tightened. My breath left me as the slide catapulted me into midair. I was hundreds of feet above the pool, now soaring in freefall, but finally in the light. Just as I felt a tinge of fear, the pool's water baptized me.

I began to weep for my prior lack of faith. My honor was in Christ, knowing that I honored Him above any earthly fear. This time, I obediently completed the steps instead of descending the stairs. As He always does, God kept me repeating the steps until I obeyed His expectation of faith.

My fear had kept me bound for many years. Yet, God never gave up on me, even when I wrapped myself in defiance and avoidance. He is faithful! Fear causes us to go the opposite way of God. When we think we are protecting ourselves, we are really hindering the fulfillment of our purpose.

This scripture bears repeating: "Such love has no fear, because perfect love expels all fear" (1 John 4:18, NLT). The power in these words describes our healing; memorize and repeat this truth often.

I had realized at this point in my life that faithful obedience is where most people struggle. I also realized that this step is never-ending and a big part of healing.

This is where we finally step out of denial in regard to an issue. We surrender control at the beginning to heal, we allow ourselves to be vulnerable, we choose to accept godly guidance, we even rid ourselves of bad roots and cycles.

But then comes obedience. It is more than a step; it is a lifestyle. We must adhere to it forever. It is another place where failure can occur because the devil knows the power in our obedience to God. This was part of his own eternal downfall; he didn't fear God. He wanted to be him, and his pride caused extreme disobedience.

Obedience has shifted the healing process in the direction of our ordained purpose in the land of do. We are allowing the Spirit to train our souls and to mold us according to God's ordination.

Let God infuse healthy, healing, loving roots into the empty places. Matthew 13:21 (NIV): "But since he has no root, he lasts only a short time. When trouble or persecution comes because of the word, he quickly falls away."

If we see and hear Him, and we learn and receive His ways, we can do His work. We can then see and ignore society's wrong methods and apply the hearing of truth to have faith for the right methods.

My mask remover, we are on a glorious journey together! I am so proud of you. You have been so faithful and so strong. Your reflection is becoming more Christlike.

These steps and awareness' begin to move us into His purpose for our lives, our part in His Kingdom work. If you do not feel quite ready to move into that yet, please rest in Him and review. We will move onto this exciting and powerful step only as He leads our growth in Him.

Congratulations! You have successfully made it up one more step and are stepping in obedience to God. You have also added another awareness to your day of fasting! You are healing and doing a great job.

Step, step, step up...up...up!

Chapter Eight

HEAR WHAT THE SPIRIT SAYS

Step Eight: Listening in Isolation with God

I pray that out of His glorious riches He may strengthen you with power through His Spirit in your inner being, so that Christ may dwell in your hearts through faith. And I pray that you, being rooted and established in love, may have power, together with all the saints, to grasp how wide and long and high and deep is the love of Christ.

Ephesians 3:16–18 (NIV)

Knowing how much He loves you allows His power in you to be widened, heightened, and deepened in exact proportion "to the measure of all the fullness of God" (Ephesians 3:19, NIV). Paul wants us to grasp this concept. God needs our time and absolute attention in order to grant us revelation on this truth. If we allow Him, He will isolate us to deepen His love in us. This is a big step and represents the last step of healing. It leads us to take steps to stay healed.

Consistent time alone with God, allowing His impartation and His Holy Spirit to touch us, is the crescendo of a healthy life. On this step, we are going to let God seal and transfer all the knowledge on the infilling of His Holy Spirit into a reality in our hearts and lives. We know how to let Him restore our soul. Now, He can teach us how to increase our spirit. So, grab hold of the horns of the altar, and let's go!

Listen for Your Healing

God has dedicated this step to making sure we understand the principles, scriptures, and concept of being filled to fullness or baptized in the Holy Spirit.

Making it up the prior steps successfully brings us to a place of purity and humility where we can begin to ascend the hill of the Lord (Psalm 24:3–5). I have purposely placed this step after obedience. In my walk, sin was so rampant, and my ignorance was so deep that until I became obedient to God's ways and not my own, I was incapable of understanding this beautiful lifeline.

God wants to fill us to a degree previously unknown to us. This fullness changes us and transforms our lives. It requires one-on-one interaction away from the distractions of life. It will require us to adjust our habits and even our schedules. He wants you to consecrate your day, your time, and your attention unto Him only for healing. The benefits far outweigh the sacrifices, but we have to give Him access to our souls to receive them.

To accept His gift, we must be vulnerable, surrendered, and free from bias. We are healing and need to allow Him to infill all the open places with truth and power. Be pure before Him. If it is not simply from Him, clear out your "religious" training. Do this in part by applying our awareness:

listening. Allow intimate isolation with God; keep it free from anticipation or supposition on your part. Embrace His expectations and reject yours.

His voice is so worthy of our discussion. Only His voice can create worlds. His voice will heal us.

When people always ask you, "How do you hear God?" Answer them in one word: listen. I found that my mother merely turned her head to the opposite side and looked more confused than ever after I finished my catalog of suggestions. I have since summed up my list into one neat word and a silent prayer for the inquisitive.

The command to listen is listed repeatedly in the Bible. Here it is in James 1:19 (NLT): "Understand this, my dear brothers and sisters: You must all be quick to listen, slow to speak, and slow to get angry." We hear God when we slow down and stop ourselves.

Our list of actions now consists of hope, faith, praying, reading, worshiping, resting, fasting, and now listening. These we need to honor and trust during our healing because they are medicine for our sickness. To listen to God means slowing down and trusting that He will speak to you.

The Smallest Room Ever

The church that housed our women's Bible study had moved to another location. It had been roughly six months from my miraculous in-filling, and we had one last meeting in the old building. I was battling fear yet again; I knew it was a big sticky gatekeeper in the healing process and knew the Lord was working on me. I followed my mentor into the elevator after class. We arrived at the first floor, and the doors opened one inch and stopped.

The elevator doors did not stop for a moment. They stopped for good. This was the exact opposite of the straight-down trip in the dark tube. In fact, it was like standing still in a lightbox and may have been even more terrifying than the tube was.

The doors did not move; not knowing when they would move again nauseated me. My blood pressure shot through the roof. Well, not literally, or we would have crawled out. If an elevator has never trapped you, it is confining, hot, and not fun.

I kept thanking God for the one-inch crack. The air was so thick inside that I felt like I was exercising just to breathe. The crack allowed us fresh air and a sense of freedom from the little box that was now our home. To be honest, it allowed me fresh air and a sense of freedom. I kept my nose pressed between the doors and was not about to move; therefore, I was the only one who could partake. We were not only at the mercy of the broken door; we were at the mercy of my selfishness.

The funny part is that my mentor was behind me as I monopolized the fresh air crack. I tried to suck all the air out of the building in a nervous fury. She stood in the back corner of the elevator phone, chit-chatting with the emergency representative in California. We were in Mississippi. The location of the tech did not encourage me. I foresaw an unknown number of hours between us and a walk in the lobby.

I pictured my mentor with her feet propped up, a pineapple drink in hand, and palm trees surrounding her. She was relaxed. She was my reference point—the "after" photo of healing. I was clearly the "before" shot; my eyeballs bulged out of the sockets, trying to see through the inch-wide crack. All the while, I crammed a crinkling Bible through the slot to ensure the crack would not close and cut off our air supply.

I was debating whether to lie down, which would eliminate the fall when I passed out in fear. In a panic, I began trying to do stuff. There is not a lot to do in a four-by-six-foot space except panic and push buttons. My mentor said, "Jennifer, you have to quit praying for alone time with me. This is getting ridiculous."

While what she said was funny and true, my unbelief, fear, and control were sad. The minute the elevator doors stuck, she grabbed hold of the lifeline, listened, and did not get off it until the trial was over. I never once grabbed onto the line. I just frantically and sporadically babbled in fear. When we are running our mouths and have no conduit, faith, or clarity, we have no connection and no ability to hear.

In that little box, God allowed me to understand that while I also possessed the very thing that I kept trying to obtain from her, I never tapped into the power for myself. I had to slow down and listen to Him to receive the power that would transition me out of constant neediness and into being healed and healing.

So often, we expect others to do stuff for us or teach us. However, God allows in us an ability to grasp and do the very thing we are waiting to receive from someone else. While He chooses to use true prophets and the gifts of the Spirit to convey information to us, the biggest part of our learning must come from listening for ourselves.

First John 2:27 says as much:

As for you, the anointing you received from Him remains in you, and you do not need anyone to teach you. But as His anointing teaches you about all things and as that anointing is real, not counterfeit—just as it has taught you, remain in Him.

1 John 2:27 (NIV)

We will take with us the authority to hear God for ourselves.

The Sweet Voice of Heaven

If we pray for alone time with God, He will meet us. It is glorious what happens in the aftermath. My daughter asked me in the sweetest voice, "Do you ever go on dates with God?" We always talk about intimacy with Christ and our Father in heaven.

"I do, precious girl, all the time," I said, waiting for her response.

"Where do you go with Him?" She really wanted to know. I could tell because she replied so fast that I could hardly make out her words.

"Well, I meet Him at church when I sing and worship; at home when I praise and pray; He is with me in the prayer room and while I am reading Scripture and studying; sometimes He shows up unexpectedly during the day when I need Him; He is with me when I run, write, work, and even when I sleep. Whenever I seek Him, He is there. He speaks to me, and I listen," I said, waiting to see a gesture of understanding.

If we do not isolate and listen to God, we will not have anything to pass on, and God wants us to pass on His love. He tells us He has set us apart, and this is good. God has segregated us from the world, and we need to let

Him teach us how and why. What we learn during our time alone with God is provision necessary for a healthy life. I am learning the importance of listening more than I speak, especially when I get angry. If we are quick to listen in our weakness, we may hear other's needs over our own and respond in love instead of hate.

I have spent countless hours isolating by reading and studying Scripture, listening to sermons, reading Christian authors, dissecting testimonies, books, and passages (many times just still listening to His voice); hours in prayer and praise; days, at times weeks, in fasting; months in waiting for Him to build my faith. He builds, tweaks, and mends, but not without our attention set upon Him, our minds free of distractions, and our ears tuned to the sweet voice of heaven. It is all worth it every moment with Him. Add glory to your life by isolating with the great *I am*.

Matthew described Jesus' focus on fellowship with God in the midst of His ministry, "After He had dismissed [the crowds], He went up on a mountainside by Himself to pray. When evening came, He was there alone" (Matthew 14:23, NIV).

Jesus spent time alone to get renewed and restored. He was in between glories. He went from feeding the 5,000 with five loaves to walking on water. In between, He needed time alone with God. After we spend time alone with God, we can step into the glory. God is the substance we need in order to perform the blessing and withstand life in a healed state.

John 6:15 (NIV) highlights the same truth: "Jesus, knowing that they intended to come and make Him king by force, withdrew again to a mountain by Himself."

John's was the most mysterious of the four Gospels. He denotes that Jesus actually retreated from the people for protection as well as restoration. If we let them, the world will try to take our purpose by force and drain us. We need to allow God to infill us to fullness; we must stay there persistently. Jesus spent a lot of time alone in prayer. We are to mimic Him:

"But when you pray, go into your room, close the door and pray to your Father, who is unseen. Then your Father, who sees what is done in secret, will reward you" (Matthew 6:6, NIV).

We do not forsake the assembly of the saints (Hebrews 10:25), but the assembly is not our sole link to God. If we are covered in the blood and full of His Spirit, we are the Church, and we should be the Church every day.

This takes discipline. Many times, discipline and isolation go hand in hand; it takes discipline to stay still enough to study or pray. I found undeniable intimacy with God when I released everything. I thought I had heard from Him for all that I knew He would yet speak. The infilling of the Holy Spirit takes listening to God. When you have intimacy and isolation with God, you need no human conduit.

Healing with the Holy Spirit

Here is the crescendo of this entire book! You have reached the pinnacle in our healing process. It is your "I have crossed the Jordan, and I am transformed" moment.

The first eight chapters have led us into God's healing and up toward His Son's likeness. The last two chapters have taught us imperative truths that readied us for this amazing moment. Now we are going to understand scripturally the truth behind the healing and healed. Then, in the last five chapters, we are going to learn and receive the glue that will bind our healing process in Jesus indefinitely.

Let us return to the baptism, or infilling, of the Holy Spirit Jesus foretold in Acts1:5. Now that we are practiced in spending quiet time with God and have an intimate relationship from listening to Him, we need to make sure we are walking in His fullness.

I am not saying that God did not fill you to overflowing upon salvation. I am not saying that He didn't fill you up three chapters back. I dare not say that you have not received it already. What I am saying is that we need to be very sensitive to the breadth of power available to us and to asking God to fill us to maximum capacity daily. We have talked about this, but we have not listened to God's Word on it yet in this book.

There are many schools of thought on this. The terms alone can provoke much controversy. I have found that I do best when I stick directly to His Word to prove my testimony. According to His Word, the blood comes first.

There are other areas, areas which He chose to leave as grey areas, in which I do not choose to have an opinion. This is not one of those. Nor do I presume that anyone needs to follow the order that I do. All I know is He took me in to know Him deeper. God made us all beautifully different, and He deals with us all perfectly differently.

I have been walking around in His circles long enough to have an understanding of many doctrinal positions on the baptism of the Holy Spirit or infilling. I have even heard of there being many fillings. The only thing I will teach is what Scripture proves true. I will leave the rest to you; you choose the vocabulary and doctrinal position as He leads you. It really doesn't matter to me what you call it as long as you get it or have it! Amen and Amen.

Sometimes, this baptism comes after salvation; it did for me. My mentor, on the other hand, received it at the point of salvation, and it grew to overflowing as she walked in her fullness. My aim is to make sure you do not live without any of the precious power God has allowed for us all.

After my salvation, I could feel the Spirit's work in my life, and at times, I allowed its strength. I did not know there was anymore of anything. So I moved into all I knew, which was not much. Yes, I could feel amazing moments of peace and joy, but I could never quite seem to "get there." When God infilled me, I still was not aware scripturally of what had occurred in my life.

Do not think that if wind and fire have never appeared in your living room, they never will. We have to remain humble and broken forever, regardless of how much time goes by, as we await His fullness. Mine took close to two decades. As long as you are saved and even if you are hurting, the fullness is available to you. If you have not obtained it, your fear may be blocking the flow.

Do not stop seeking and asking for it (Luke 11:9). Remain, and He will fulfill His promise to you. His promise is written in His Word (Luke 24:49). He never changes, and neither do His promises. Hebrews 13:8 (NIV) says, "Jesus Christ is the same yesterday and today and forever." Sometimes, the fullness comes twenty years after salvation. The fulfillment of the promise is related to our surrender and God's order.

Here are three examples of the baptism of the Holy Spirit from the Book of Acts (there are many examples throughout the New Testament):

Peter replied, "Repent and be baptized, every one of you, in the name of Jesus Christ for the forgiveness of your sins. And you will receive the gift of the Holy Spirit. The promise is for you and your children and for all who are far off—for all whom the Lord our God will call."

Acts 2:38–39 (NIV)

When [Peter and John] arrived, they prayed for [the Samaritan believers] that they might receive the Holy Spirit, because the Holy Spirit had not yet come upon any of them; they had simply been baptized into the name of the Lord Jesus. Then Peter and John placed their hands on them, and they received the Holy Spirit.

Acts 8:15–17 (NIV)

In Acts 10:46–47 (NIV), we see: "Peter said, 'Can anyone keep these people from being baptized with water? They have received the Holy Spirit just as we have.'" This example teaches us not to presume that everyone must follow a certain order to receive the fullness. The point is that God poured out His Spirit for all. We need the fullness of His Spirit at some point during our journey to stay healthy and walk in freedom.

You know you are walking in His fullness and are infilled when you begin to change. The things of this world become less appealing, and the things of God become your necessities.

Hearing God comes naturally. You notice a new understanding of Scripture. Prayer will become like breathing, isolation with God—a requirement. Bless you, my sweet friends. Be filled with all the fullness of the Lord!

Amazing Grace

God's greatest moments are seen in our weakness. That is where God's power works best. This was a truth the apostle Paul knew well:

[Jesus] said, "My grace is all you need. My power works best in weakness." So now I [Paul] am glad to boast about my weaknesses, so that the power of Christ can work through me. That's why I take pleasure in my weaknesses, and in the insults, hardships, persecutions, and troubles that I suffer for Christ. For when I am weak, then I am strong.

2 Corinthians 12:9–10 (NLT)

Your testimony is born in your weakness.

We sometimes want to give up right before the trumpet blasts. If we will press a little further, He will heal us. Listen. Listen. Listen to His voice and, in the stillness, receive.

Let us praise Him, saying, "Thank You, precious God, for speaking to us and for granting us the ability to hear You. Thank You for infilling us with the fullness of your Holy Spirit. Thank you for isolating us and giving us second and third chances to get it right!"

Are you ready to receive the glue that will bind your healthy life to Christ's for endurance in your healed and healing state? God created you for a mighty purpose, hope, and a future. You can look at fear, quote Scripture, and reside in faith because you, my friend, are walking into power on the next step.

These remaining steps are less about our actions and more about allowing God to impart His power and transform us into His Son's image. We are stepping into a new section where we will learn how to stay healthy for life. These steps are imperative. You are transitioning into what I call "the stamina stairs."

Congratulations!

When we are humble, broken, and surrendered, He can then baptize us into the fullness of His Holy Spirit. You have successfully made it into isolation with the Father and taken another step. You have added a new awareness: listening! Before we go on to the next step, let's do an important study.

The Baptism (Infilling) of the Holy Spirit (Acts 1:5)

Again, we do not presume that everyone's experience with the infilling must follow a certain order or experience. God poured His Spirit out for all.

We need the fullness of His Spirit; He will give it to us at some point during our journey to walk in freedom.

Meditate on the scriptures below that we touched on previously; this time, underline the order of water baptism versus Spirit baptism. Jot down the orders and how they differentiate. Then journal what a broken Spirit and a contrite heart mean to you (Psalm 51:17):

Peter replied, "Repent and be baptized, every one of you, in the name of Jesus Christ for the forgiveness of your sins. And you will receive the gift of the Holy Spirit. The promise is for you and your children and for all who are far off—for all whom the Lord our God will call."

Acts 2:38–39 (NIV)

When [Peter and John] arrived, they prayed for [the Samaritan believers] that they might receive the Holy Spirit, because the Holy Spirit had not yet come upon any of them; they had simply been baptized into the name of the Lord Jesus. Then Peter and John placed their hands on them, and they received the Holy Spirit.

Acts 8:15–17 (NIV)

"Then Peter said, 'Can anyone keep these people from being baptized with water? They have received the Holy Spirit just as we have'"

(Acts 10:46–47, NCV)

Just a few things the Holy Spirit does in our life:

> » Convicts the world of sin, righteousness, and judgment (John 16:8–11);

> » Guides us into all truth (John 16:13);

> » Glorifies Christ (John 16:14);

> » Marks us and seals us (Ephesians 1:13–14;

> » 2 Corinthians 2:20–22);

> » Christ in us (John 16:14–15);

> » Gives us the mind of Christ (1 Corinthians 2);

> » Leads and teaches us (1 John 2:20 and 27);

> » Sanctifies, restores, regenerates, renews us (Romans 8);

> » Empowers us (Acts 1:8; 1 Corinthians 4:20);

> » Fills us (Ephesians 5:18);

> » Teaches us to pray (Romans 8:26–27; 1 Corinthians 14:15);

> » Tells us that we are children of God and that we share in His glory (Romans 8:16–17);

> » Produces the fruit of the Spirit in us (Galatians 5:22– 23);

> » Gives us special supernatural gifts (1 Corinthians 12:8–10);

Take a look at these scriptures and pray for revelation:

And I will ask the Father, and He will give you another Counselor to be with you forever—the Spirit of truth. The world cannot accept Him, because it neither sees Him nor knows Him. But you know Him, for He lives with you and will be in you.

John 14:16–1 (NIV) (emphasis added)

"I am going to send you what My Father has promised; but stay in the city until you have been clothed with power from on high"

(Luke 24:49, NIV)

When the day of Pentecost came, they were all together in one place. Suddenly, a sound like the blowing of a violent wind came from heaven and filled the whole house where they were sitting. They saw what seemed to be tongues of fire that separated and came to rest on each of them. All of them were filled with the Holy Spirit and began to speak in other tongues as the Spirit enabled them

(Acts 2:1–4)

There is also a prayer language that accompanies this truth. I did not know this when I was baptized, and with my controlling type, nature did not allow my tongue to relax enough, I am sure. Therefore, I had to tarry for it or ask for my gift. It is the ability to talk to God unhindered by the enemy, and it goes directly to the throne of grace. It builds up your Spirit. A few scripture references are Romans 8:26–27, 1 Corinthians 2:13 and 14:15, Mark 16:17, and Acts 2:4 above:

For this reason, I kneel before the Father, from whom his whole family in heaven and on earth derives its name. I pray that out of his glorious riches he may strengthen you with power through his Spirit in your inner being, so that Christ may dwell in your hearts through faith. And I pray that you, being rooted and established in love, may have power, together with all the saints, to grasp how wide and long and high and deep is the love of Christ, and to know this love that surpasses knowledge—that you may be filled to the measure of all the fullness of God. Now to him who is able to do immeasurably more than all we ask or imagine, according to his power that is at work within us, to him be glory in the church and in Christ Jesus throughout all generations, forever and ever! Amen.

Ephesians 3:14–21(NIV)

Before you step on, please ask for this mighty power and know that I have prayed and believe for you already.

Congratulations! You are now headed into balance for your steps and are about to step into God's fruit. We have studied on the infilling, and we are stepping in or at least toward authority and freedom, so step up.

Chapter Nine

WIELDING YOUR SCEPTER WITH BALANCE

Step Nine: God's Balance Through Giving

"Be well balanced (temperate, sober of mind), be vigilant and cautious at all times; for that enemy of yours, the devil, roams around like a lion roaring [in fierce hunger], seeking someone to seize upon and devour"

(1 Peter 5:8 AMP)

The Rat of Imbalance

We are the ones who limit God because we do not believe in His abundance and fullness. We are going to step up into God's measure and allow His completeness to balance us. God will counterbalance our chemically imbalanced pain with His steadying hand. His love is the antidote for our unnecessary reactions to adversity.

It was one of those moments. Awakened by the sound, I glanced toward the clock. The neon numbers read 3:00. The scratching that awakened me was coming from inside our bedroom.

I asked my first husband, "Do you hear that?" I was not comfortable sleeping with a rodent in the same room. Not to mention, our three-month-old baby was nestled next to me.

"Hello?"

He rolled over and said, "I'll kill it in the morning."

"Okay, great! I'm sure it heard you and will stand real still till you are done with your coffee and paper. Perfect," I said.

I froze in fear. This reaction always happened. When fear came, the muscles locked up. I would not move. I just kept thinking, *If I touch my foot to the floor, that thing is going to come into contact with me.*

Chills and an itchy tingle made me twitch. The scratching did not cease. Even the addition of our voices to the quiet of the room did not hinder the thing. I lay awake all night listening to gauge its whereabouts. The thing was under the bed at one point. The clock ticked rather slowly.

Finally, the window's silhouette showed up out of the darkness. The sun came up, and with it, the revelation of what the scratching had produced: a hole in the wall with droppings all around it. I began to investigate. I found the signs of an infestation. I saw droppings all over the house: in the cupboards, bathrooms, couch cushions, even the baby's room. In my mind, the problem could not possibly be just one rodent.

My first husband just got up and left town for several weeks, leaving me alone with the pack of rats. I was desperate and dramatic. This was not okay with me, not okay at all. The rodents were like big fuzzy roaches to me; they were just as fast, just as nasty. I was already writing *The Mask of Ratatouille* in my mind.

My imagination had them reproducing for months, and I had just slept through it all. They are nocturnal. Therefore, their schedule had not crossed my schedule till now. I was oblivious and had convinced myself that one little rodent could not have done this much damage. We are so easily deceived.

From my reign as the Maskquerade Queen, I knew exactly what to do: traps! I bought glue traps, snap traps, and poison traps, employed a pest trapper, called in relatives to trap the rodents, and invited some trapping friends to help. I lined the room with the mechanisms. I surrounded the bed, pantry, and attic with them. My house was filled with them. Everywhere I saw a dropping, I stationed a solution.

My mom flew in with panther urine, a supposed cure. That would be logical in some countries; if a rodent thought a panther was nearby, it probably would not want to stick around too long. But do American rodents innately know this? If panthers are not indigenous to, say, a subdivision in Mississippi, would the rodent know enough to run?

Not only were we doused in exotic animal urine, I had already made contact with the health department. I had a bad cold, but I was sure it was from exposure to bacteria from the unknown number of rats surrounding me as I slept. I will not even bore you with the steel wool and duct tape episode. Suffice it to say, I am still pulling it out of crevices.

Weeks passed. One night, before leaving for church to help head up a ministry called "Lifehouse," I pulled the decorative pillows off the back of our bed to wash them. What do you think I found? Right above the place where my sweet baby slept, there were droppings! I went into freak-out mode, an imbalanced approach to fixing anything.

I stripped the bed. I called the ministry folk and told them I had a war to fight and would not be joining them. I said, "Please pray for us."

My plight was not entirely uncommon. I know almost everyone has had the odd rodent drop in. But it flipped me out. I wanted to pop a tent up on the roof to sleep at night; thankfully, things never quite got that insane.

The battle was over when I finally told God I trusted Him for the outcome. That night, I slept instead of playing night watchman. His hand was seen. The next morning, one tiny, spotted mouse sat wiggling on a glue trap. That was it! I realized that I had likely imagined my home to be the site of Armageddon—all because of one little mouse.

My measure had been way off. I had traps everywhere. Until I allowed God to reveal His measure, I was a mess and extremely out of balance. You can imagine me getting the paper in the morning in a beekeeper's suit with mousetraps dangling from a tool belt and a broom in my hand. I was worn out from sleep deprivation. The slightest wind would send me jumping. I had allowed one small mouse to imbalance my whole life for two weeks.

This example is silly, I know. But I am not kidding when I say that I was not right those two weeks. I could not function. My reactions were out of balance from the fear of one tiny mouse. He was ruling my life.

Our heightened, imbalanced reactions to pain are the fleshly responses the devil loves. We must step toward God in prayer and worship to stay steady. God never intended for us to allow our circumstances to control us and throw us out of balance. He is, after all, the One who controls even the wind.

In our weakness and sickness, our gasping for breath and allowing things to overwhelm us is expected. Once we have proper coping mechanisms and God in our lives to buffer the fear, such reactions are senseless. We are merely letting one tiny demon rule us.

When we view issues through the eyes of faith, knowing that God is in total control, we are measuring life's situations using God's ruler. That keeps us balanced.

God's measure is vast. Paul tells us in Ephesians 3:8 that His power at work within us is immeasurable. He also talks about our being filled to the measure of all the fullness of God. In Ephesians 4:13, he talks about the full measure of Christ in regard to our unity and our service to the Body of Christ.

When God fills us with His Spirit, the measure of power we can tap into becomes limitless. When we tap that measure, He balances us. That measure is a measure of faith, peace, and joy during times of infestation or solo varmint issues. This measure is beyond sufficient to produce serenity in the midst of chaos. We rely on God to engage His fruit and balance our lives so that we stand when all else is falling. In fact, His balance is so stabilizing and so abundant that we can even step up when all else is declining.

In our prior step, as we reveled in God's isolation, we were made ready for this bountiful stair. We will never feel totally prepared, but we are ready. We know that we are not capable without His Spirit in us. With His Spirit in us, we might fall (as I did), but we get right back up, dust ourselves off, and keep stepping (Proverbs 24:16). We do not allow the enemy to hinder our healing.

More Blessed to Give

We are stepping up into giving, which will add to our healing. We needed to heal before we could help. Once we have committed to healing, we can begin to pour into others. When we pour out, we feel God pouring more in, and we realize that we are healing even more. God's measure of healing will increase as we allow it to flow outward.

When I get down and feel like I am sad, Jesus always says, "Get your blood covering on, pray, invite the Spirit back in, and go help someone. Go minister, give, and serve. Get out of yourself."

I was almost two years into healing when my pastor's wife asked me to start a healing ministry in our church. I stared at her for an undisclosed length of time and then took a breath. I realized I had not breathed for quite a while. I did not want to startle her by turning blue.

When God speaks to her, she fulfills His requests. Leadership had asked me a year earlier to head up a similar group. That leadership left when the church broke, and the group was never established. God did not stop asking. Once everything was reestablished, His request was declared again.

I, however, did not want to be responsible for a group. The Lord took me to 2 Corinthians 8:10–11:

Here is my advice: It would be good for you to finish what you started a year ago. Last year you were the first who wanted to give, and you

were the first to begin doing it. Now you should finish what you started.
Let the eagerness you showed in the beginning be matched now by your
giving. Give in proportion to what you have.

2 Corinthians 8:10–11 (NLT)

Lifehouse was born. It was a healing ministry for sin issues. I had been professing my mask of pain that Christ overcame, but being asked to help others was foreign to me. My heart was selflessly in love with Christ, so His passion became my passion. I got involved as a way of giving back; what I realized a year later was that what I had put in had come back to me beyond measure.

Because I knew my sin nature was to serve myself, I had to serve others. This allowed God to train my ways to serve Him. My sacrifice to service allowed God to create balance in my life. Second Corinthians 1:4–5 says:

God the Father comforts us in all our troubles, so that we can comfort
those in any trouble with the comfort we ourselves have received from
God. For just as the sufferings of Christ flow over into our lives, so also
through Christ our comfort overflows.

2 Corinthians 1:4–5 (NIV)

He had pressed down blessing and healing, shaken them together, and poured them running over into our laps. God used that beautiful ministry and all of its precious leaders to heal us. We were willing, humble, and open. We all received beyond measure. Luke 6:38 (NIV) explains, "Give, and it will be given to you. A good measure, pressed down, shaken together and running over, will be poured into your lap. For with the measure you use, it will be measured to you."

We are finding understanding about the balance in our lives by allowing God to impose His standards of measurement. Job 31:5–6 (KJV): "If I have walked with vanity, or if my foot hath hasted to deceit; let me be weighed in an even balance that God may know mine integrity." His measure teaches us proper balance and function within the boundaries of grace.

Left Brain, Right Brain

Most of us are being ruled either by the right brain or the left. Right-brainers are spontaneous, creative people. They are purpose-oriented, poetic visionaries who work best with others. Left-brainers are logical, task-oriented, goal-oriented, and technical people who work best alone.

In order to flow freely in God's will, we must allow Him to merge the left and right sides of our minds. We can allow God to transform our minds and create the minds of Christ in us. We can pray for Him to enlarge the territory we use in our minds and give us more of a capacity to understand Him, His ways, and His Word.

In our fleshly state, we are allergic to God's balance. God attributes balance to integrity in Job 31:5–6 (NIV): "If I have walked in falsehood or my foot has hurried after deceit—let God weigh me in honest scales and He will know that I am blameless."

God honors those who honor Him. Unfortunately, most of us are unbalanced. You often hear people complaining about balancing the checkbook, the scale, their opinions with others, or their schedules. The Lord holds the power of balance. We can only attain it through the cross of Christ. Without salvation and the infilling of the Holy Spirit, godly balance is a rabbit we can never catch.

The imbalance produced in our sickness literally tilted us. I like to think our struggle with equilibrium results from having a foot on one step with the other attempting to step too soon or in the opposite direction. We just cannot seem to commit. Even our churches seem to be out of balance. We have heavy "Word" churches or "too spiritual" churches. Revelation 2 depicts the absence of balance. Without His Spirit and His truth, we are imbalanced. We are crooked at best; without Christ, our feet walk a crooked path toward destruction.

The cross represents perfect balance, physically speaking, from east to west. In the cross, God perfectly balanced justice and mercy; both are satisfied and fulfilled. Extreme emotional turmoil is the opposite of God's plumb line. His line rests in righteousness between calm and peace. James even tells us in 3:18 that peacemakers who sow in peace will reap a harvest of righteousness.

Balance is important as we step up. We realize this is where the permanence in our healing is found. Balance will keep us away from the extremes that pull us back into sickness. When we realize that balance is God's, we begin to appropriate it for our lives. The first place I felt it was in my emotions. God balanced my feelings into a peaceful state.

Before He blessed me with the fullness of the Holy Spirit, I was up and down on an emotional roller coaster. I allowed satan to jerk and manipulate me at the slightest provocation. The enemy uses our emotions to control us. Even after I came out of some healing, I became too legalistic in my left-brained ways. I had to let Him guide my thoughts away from the left side and over to the right a little, hence the rewriting of the former book, *The Roach Princess.* It is amazing how we are constantly changing and if we allow amalgamating with Christ.

We do not want to be something we are not; we just tend to be too much of what we choose sometimes and not enough of what God intended us to be.

The Devil Came to Kill Me

I did not know he was watching me. My friends and I were careless in the last years of high school. The sidewalks we trod led through some dark alleys and turnstiles most people would avoid. I was chemically imbalanced from alcohol and depression. My unstable emotions caused me to make life-threatening decisions. Sometimes, in our pain, we think we want to die. I was about to, had the angels not intervened.

My friend and I wandered the streets of Atlanta, in and out of all the bars. Our last stop on a particular night was a shady, back-alley pool hall where a predator was hanging out. Whether satan had assigned him specifically to me or not, my sickness and addiction had tilted me enough to fall prey to his attack. I was intoxicated, unaware, and unguarded.

The rain came down in sheets as we left the smoke-filled bar. Thunder cracked, and lightning lit up the street periodically, allowing us to see in front of the car. What was behind us went unnoticed. The predator was there following us, not too close and not too far.

The methodical beat of the alternative music from the dash was haunting. My friend turned the steering wheel and maneuvered the station wagon down the long, winding driveway. It curved around a ravine and up into the thick woods. The house was dark; no one was home. The thunder rumbled; it sounded as if God was not pleased. I was dizzy from the alcohol and beginning to get sleepy. I stepped out of the car and shivered as the cold rain hit my skin and sobered me a little.

"See you later. Be careful driving home," I hollered as I ran for the protection of my parents' carport. The predator was watching from the protection of the woods as my friend pulled away. Alone, I entered the house. I noticed the lightning had turned off the alarm; it was an old system that would shut down when storms affected the electricity. The green light was all that I could see in the darkness. I entered my house, locked the door, and reset the alarm.

The house was so dark that I tripped upon entering. I flipped a switch to navigate and headed for my bed. I was dizzy from drinking all evening and almost sick. I remember sitting on my bed, listening to the storm and worrying. Worry was one of the operating habits I had formed from the lifestyle that I was using to escape my pain.

I did not even know a predator was standing at the back door waiting for the right moment. The power failed again, disengaging the alarm. Instead of waiting for the alarm to come back on, I felt my way into my father's room and reached into the top drawer. My fingers welcomed the hard, cold metal buried in the soft socks. I gripped the gun properly and pulled it out. As I turned, I heard breaking glass hit the hardwood floor in another part of the house.

The back French doors were in the living room, just one room over. They creaked open. I could hear the thunder and rain as though it were inside the house. The movement I heard was not the storm. Someone was in the house with me. My stomach felt like it had crawled up into my chest. Breath was hard to draw in.

I went into fight-or-flight mode but realized that I would have to reside in fight if I wanted to make it to flight. I began to make my way down the narrow hallway to the living room. Everything became surreal. I calculated my steps in the darkness. My goal was safety. When death came knocking, I suddenly wanted to live.

As I turned the corner, the moonlight illuminated a man entering the living room. I could feel evil. I lifted the gun and cocked it. I will never forget the pressure of the trigger against my fingertip. I had the power to pull his very life out of his body with one motion.

My mind could not even conceptualize the magnitude of the moment. Seeing the pistol and realizing his fate, he lunged toward me. I faced a life-and-death choice. I like to think since God knew I was incapable of making such a weighty decision, He pardoned me.

My ears rang as the gun fired. The rain and thunder went unheard. I believe that, at that moment, God changed my hearing forever; I know my life was altered. The intruder could have raped me and then killed me.

I was blessed enough not to have killed him. I do not even know where he went in that moment or whether God took him away. I made it to my car and to my mother's home. She then called law enforcement. The police took care of the predator's whereabouts from there. A week later, the cat and dog ended up dead on our lawn, but I went unscathed. We knew it was him, but he was never caught, not yet bound.

I didn't think that I led the predator there; I did not realize that I had until years later. My friends and I ran around the back alleys of a big city. We never expected foul play around us. Our imbalances put us in jeopardy of making bad choices.

But now, you and I have a new ability to let God merge our minds and balance them. He will give us the capability to make sound choices that will protect our lives and healing.

If most cats have nine lives, I have ten. In all truth, I did have ten of God's fingers wrapped around me at all times. An act of God on behalf of an unworthy sinner—how often it occurs. The bullet struck also ten feet from the doorframe where the man stood. No one could have heard the shot. Because the bullet did not hit him and because I was temporarily deafened by the blast (and shocked overall), the predator could have finished me off. He had free reign to do so, but God's reign is still freer.

Before I discovered my antonym theory, I began to pray that God would reveal specific ways to improve my responses to stress. When I became frustrated, I would ask, "God, what word or action can turn this feeling away before it leads into anger?"

He told me to go find a treasure in His Word to combat the flesh response. He knew my personality; He knew I was a treasure hunter who would use the awareness I stumbled upon and give it to others.

That is when I really began to understand how to use His Word as a weapon. When you find wisdom and realize it counterbalances weak behavior, you have found a cure. I meditated on Proverbs 19:11 (NIV): "A man's wisdom gives him patience; it is to his glory to overlook an offense."

I realized the antonym to frustration is satisfaction. The minute the first syllable left my tongue, I knew that was my issue. I was not struggling with frustration. I was struggling with an imbalance; my expectations were skewed between wanting to serve and being served. Often, the answer to healing is found in the counterbalanced sides of an issue. We must search for the remedy in the Bible. We need to be satisfied that we have breath. If we are serving with an expectation of servanthood, we are safe from frustration.

I do not know why, but I am always flabbergasted when a rocky road ends in a cool, calm lake of simplicity. I love intricate revelations of wisdom; I enjoy figuring out complex issues. In the final analysis, however, the most profound and life-changing things are simple. True satisfaction is an impossible feat without godly balance, giving to counterbalance self and God's wisdom.

We are never hopeless with Christ. We may feel that way at times, but He loves us and remembers us. Our trials are for His glory. Step for Him in and out of your pain, even if it seems impossible. We are stepping higher, but we are still human. We need to keep our physical and spiritual expectations balanced.

That is where we are heading to...balance. We are obedient, full, and allowing God to balance everything. We need to grab hold of our Vine, Jesus Christ; the Vine will impart balance and sturdiness in our lives. We also reach for the handrail of godly relationships to steady us and lead us forward.

God's fruit produces life—in our lives and in others as we give and serve others (serving is our next level of awareness). Godly fruit brings healing in our lives and through our lives to others.

In a powerful passage from the Gospel of John, Jesus teaches us how godly fruit is born:

> *I am the true vine, and My Father is the gardener. He cuts off every branch in Me that bears no fruit, while every branch that does bear fruit He prunes so that it will be even more fruitful. You are already clean because of the word I have spoken to you. Remain in me, and I will remain in you. No branch can bear fruit by itself; it must remain in the vine. Neither can you bear fruit unless you remain in Me. I am the vine; you are the branches. If a man remains in Me and I in him, he will bear much fruit; apart from Me you can do nothing.*
>
> John 15:1–5 (NIV)

We must "remain." He says this word more than a dozen times in John 15. He tells us that we can do nothing apart from Him. We cannot balance our emotionalism without Him.

If you notice, God's fruit is the opposite of our emotions. Antonyms reveal the dichotomy: The opposite of peace is worry. The reverse of self-control is rudeness. The opposite of gentleness is brutality. The opposite of hate is love. We can step up knowing that God's fruit is the remedy for our chemical imbalance.

God's fruit brings spiritual satisfaction, just as physical fruit pleases the physical body and senses. My stomach growled at the nauseous feeling. A lack of food had plunged me into a sugar imbalance, making it difficult to do my work. Dizzy from hunger, I made my way over to the fruit bowl and lifted out a white peach. I rinsed it and took a bite. The juice and sweetness were satisfying.

In that instant, I could relate to God's spiritual fruit. It was the "medicine" my out-of-balance soul needed. The sense of satisfaction gained from serving others was becoming evident. The connection was settling into my mind. It is time to step up with our newfound balance. Our fruit baskets are about to become full; we don't want them to tip over and spill God's precious remedy.

I told you this step would be less about our actions and more about allowing God's impartation of power to transform us into the image of Christ—balanced and willing to give, make us healthy for life. This step and the coming steps of impartation are critical to your staying healed.

Congratulations! You are balanced! You have also added the awareness of giving. Keep stepping mask remover; step up into His fruit.

Chapter Ten

VINEYARD BY THE CASTLE COURT

Step Ten: God's Fruit Gives Us a Servant's Heart

"But the fruit of the Spirit is love, joy, peace, patience, kindness, goodness, faithfulness, gentleness and self-control"

(Galatians 5:22–23, NIV)

We are not naturally of noble character. In fact, we often label ourselves "Christian" without giving enough thought to what it means. We think the label alone will cover our actions. Grace makes healing available; our choices make healing possible. Stepping in His will dictates our blessings and will keep us healthy. Living for God and being healed is not about outward appearances.

A healthy life is about what God has done on the inside through the blood of His Son and His Spirit. People will know He lives in us when they see His love and His fruit operating in our lives. According to Matthew 7:17, fruit is either good or bad; it cannot be both. We will produce God's fruit when we are ready to serve Him and others first.

Galatians 5 talks at about the fruit of the Spirit. These fruit are not manifested through our natural physical efforts. Galatians 5:25 (NIV) makes that clear: "Since we live by the Spirit, let us keep in step with the Spirit."

As we step up in spirit and in truth, we heal. The temple stairs that we are climbing trail beneath the torn curtain and into the Holy of Holies as we manifest God's functioning fruit to provide stability for our healing journey. We are to be "fruitful trees," blessed and producing the fruit of God's choosing.

Fruitlessness is contrary to God's ways, as Jesus demonstrated:

In the morning, as Jesus was returning to Jerusalem, He was hungry, and He noticed a fig tree beside the road. He went over to see if there were any figs, but there were only leaves. Then He said to it, "May you never bear fruit again!" And immediately the fig tree withered up.

Matthew 21:18–19 (NLT)

We need blossoms on our fig tree and grapes on our vine. John the Baptist said in Matthew 3:8 to "produce fruit in keeping with repentance." Our godly sorrow in repentance keeps us in His grace; our fruit keeps us moving forward.

We so often connect man's morality and performance with God's fruitfulness. However, man's principles often produce bondage and perfectionism. The plan of satan is to keep us feeling like we need to achieve salvation. We know better: we know that salvation is received because of grace, not performance, but then we confuse ourselves, thinking the rest will be just as easy.

We have thrown off the hindrances to healing, including performance mentality. Now, we must take on those things that will assist us in staying healthy. We do not need to perform "a song and dance" in order to feel like we are of noble enough character to call ourselves Christians. God sees our hearts. He wants full access, not a front-row seat to a fake fruit extravaganza. If we are seeking Him in obedience and allowing Him to access our hearts, our fruit will blossom in His time. Just as is true with balance, the fruit will come from Him only.

Now that we are successfully stepping up into this divine promise, we must understand that we are not miraculously going to produce superior character at once. It is not ours to manufacture but to receive through intimacy with God.

Just as was true with obedience, we become what we see, hear, learn, accept as truth, and do. This infiltration and initiation become how we live and, eventually, who we are. We know enough to protect our children from the world, yet we allow society to infiltrate our hearts with death every day. We must arrest this process, as our ingestion will eventually affect our children and the world around us.

I operated in the opposite of the fruit for so long that when God began to change me, my new character was suddenly foreign to me. We cannot expect God to heal others through us if we are constantly trying to be something we feel we are not. We have to allow God to genuinely make us these things and accept His ways. Fake fruit will not change hearts.

We look for the fruit, but we cannot assume that because kindness looks good at church, it is God's fruit. My grandma used to have plastic grapes on her kitchen table: they looked like real grapes; they even felt like real grapes, but they were just rubber.

Our true fruit surfaces behind closed doors, where no one is watching. Fruit does not need an audience or applause. True fruit comes from a seed that goes into the ground alone in the dark and then dies before it becomes what God intended. All the glory, honor, and praise to Him.

Fruit before Gifts

As we regain spiritual health and balance, we realize we are sensitive to those who are still hurting. We will love them enough to descend to the base of the temple stairs for their sake. We help them by gently nudging them upward and not judging them for their weakness. Let us remember it was in our weakness that God met and healed us.

On this tenth step, we begin to realize that we are healing and healthy enough to begin serving. To obtain a true servant's heart, we must serve from the place of purity rather than capacity.

That is why we are accepting this awareness before we know our spiritual gifts. Please sweet friend, never allow anyone to make you feel like you are not worthy to serve the King of kings and Lord of lords. Serving helps establish fruit in our lives; the fruit of the Spirit must be established before we exhibit the gifts. At every stage of the process, we pray for faith, fruit, and wisdom.

So many want the blessings, but so few want to do the work. So few are willing to climb upward to find what we are seeking. Healing unto serving is not a quick fix; this action takes ridding ourselves of self. Selflessness is blessed, and every step in servanthood to Christ brings us closer to heaven, where God's truths and love reside (Romans 12).

The Service of Our Life

As we ascend, we feel the reverberation of the angels dancing about the throne of God, singing, "Holy, holy, holy is the Lord Almighty; the whole earth is full of His glory" (Isaiah 6:3). Revelation 4:8 (NIV) describes the Lord God Almighty as the One "Who was, and is, and is to come." As we get closer to Him, we truly can feel His love, joy, and peace.

Too often, we are motivated by the desire to see the blessing. I always try to keep my mind focused on eternity. We cannot have worldly expectations and live a healthy, godly life. Our expectations need to be focused on servanthood. I am repeating this truth because our flesh wants to do the exact opposite, and pure, humble servanthood, in its essence, heals, delivers, and sets us free.

Jesus did not seek recognition. He did not flaunt His power or draw attention to Himself as a means of stroking His ego. He was focused on the reality of eternity and the needs of people:

When He saw the crowds, He had compassion on them because they were confused and helpless, like sheep without a shepherd. He said to His disciples, "The harvest is great, but the workers are few. So pray to the Lord who is in charge of the harvest; ask Him to send more workers into His fields."

Matthew 9:36–38 (NLT)

Several years after my initial transformation, I was asked to speak at an outdoor worship service. Speaking and teaching were terrifying to me at this level, but I was called to serve regardless of my comfort zone. I had to rely on His comfort, and that is where a true servant is born, out of his comfort zone. If you aren't growing in your comfort zone, step out and serve. The overcoming helps, I promise, because now I am okay, speaking and teaching, but it took a lot of serving first.

I went to the location prior to praying, and, looking out on the most glorious field, I noticed that the wheat glowed as if the sun was shining out from within. A blanket of mist hovered above the luminous harvest. I wept and prayed as it reminded me of His church and the covering of the Spirit. I was so new to the experience that I did not understand what part was God's and what part was mine. I do now; it's all His, and all of it is for His glory, which is servanthood!

God impressed upon me just how plentiful His harvest was to be and how few were in place to bring the harvest into the Kingdom. Therefore, I took my cue from Mark 9, praying for one more worker with every step I took. I must have walked a mile that morning. The mantle of fog was His Holy Spirit hovering about His wheat. That evening, I asked the crowd to work for Him in power without holding back.

We are to produce fruit in increasing measure. We cannot fill a need unless seed is planted. If the only place we are professing Christ is in our church pews, we may not be working the totality of our harvest. The unsaved are hurting, as we once were and are at times. Do you remember your life without Christ? Does your heart ache for the harvest? Fruit abounds when healing takes root, and God's love becomes our ultimate motivation.

Months prior to this experience, God deposited the vision of a community-wide women's group, the template for The Way for The Wayward. He showed me a group of women from all different churches and denominations who would strengthen one another and vow to go out and work the harvest from a Kingdom perspective with power from on high. "As iron sharpens iron, so a friend sharpens a friend" (Proverbs 27:17, NLT).

Our first year, we read the Word straight through (Appendix A) and studied the deep foundational truths from Genesis to Revelation. We met regardless of the weather, schedules, and pleasures. We stayed on the narrow path, and we have seen God's glory for it. The group is actually a seedbed for a much larger structure that I hope will spread across the nation; one whose agenda is purely to seek after the Father's heart.

My prayers are that God will lead me to press on with The Way, whatever that may be for Him. This particular service helped me further my healing. Service to assist others to fashion their lives for the cause of Christ will keep us healthy. Keep stepping and know there is always more glorious riches in His Kingdom for us to attain to.

We are gaining understanding of the fruit, and we are learning to distinguish them from their opposites. When we stroll down the rotten produce aisle of satan's grocery store, we will accurately identify the ailments we see. Let us move with fresh oil toward the lamp that lights the path to God's produce aisle. Jesus wants to use us to save a part of His harvest.

Fruit Is Our Protection

As we heal and learn, we become fruitful and accept the call to servanthood. We begin to flow upward in more of a glide than a pulse, moving seamlessly by the Holy Spirit. Our stepping up is becoming more fluid, almost like an elevator in motion. Love, joy, and peace are coming down from heaven into and through our lives.

"For the Kingdom of God is not a matter of what we eat or drink, but of living a life of goodness and peace and joy in the Holy Spirit" (Romans 14:17, NLT).

God is honing our character; we are becoming more Christlike with each day. This equipping for service helps us to produce fruit in keeping with His desire:

> *For this very reason, make every effort to add to your faith goodness; and to goodness, knowledge; and to knowledge, self-control; and to self-control, perseverance; and to perseverance, godliness; and to godliness, brotherly kindness; and to brotherly kindness, love. For if you possess these qualities in increasing measure, they will keep you from being ineffective and unproductive in your knowledge of our Lord Jesus Christ.*

2 Peter 1:5–8 (NIV)

When these things begin to increase, they will help us to be more productive in our service. In the above passage, Peter names some of the fruit of the Spirit. Self-control is a quality only the Spirit knows in its perfection. Here, the Spirit presents it in relation to knowledge and perseverance, showing us how these qualities work together in us. In fact, that scripture is abounding in information; look deeper into the order in which each principle is placed, and a powerful sermon/bible study could erupt from that scripture.

Many times, Christ's kindness doesn't look kind (in our terms) but tough. We need to be careful not to use human kindness to enable others to sin. We need to pray and allow God to give us His actions and reactions. Now that we are healthy, we need to practice restraining our flesh by crucifying our desires or bad fruit.

Sometimes, godly kindness means refraining from doing the things we think will help. Kindness, self-control, and gentleness remind me of my husband, Sam. He is so Christlike and full of fruit that he amazes me more each day. What a blessing to live with that kind of example. We must judge kindness and any other trait or fruit by godly standards.

The nature of secular kindness often lies in emotionalism; often, our kindness is gauged by the level of personal satisfaction the doling out of kindness brings to us. Sam operates for others first, out of a servant's heart of humility. It is of no use to look and act "kind" while we ignore God's promptings, refuse to read His Word, and fail to call on Him as He asks us to do.

Satan was the leader of worship in God's Kingdom. He was a beautiful angel in heaven. He fell because he allowed himself to be reduced to a prideful, selfish evil. He was tossed out of heaven and landed among us. Goodness, kindness, and every other godly quality are easily counterfeited on this earth.

In order to deceive, a counterfeit must look, to the naked eye, exactly like the original. We must be keen to discern and jump from our fear to succeed in letting God set us free! Worldly goodness has implications of a degree of excellence. What is important is resurrecting our goodness to that which is in Christ Jesus. I thought getting divorced would be too sinful for God and that I would be making the wrong choice, yet my marriage was making me sick, taking ministry and life from me.

When we are sick and hurting, our godly fruit remains unexpressed and hidden in our hearts. This is true of goodness. We settle for the secular version of goodness that is easily accepted but not pleasing to God because it is not based on truth. We should not and do not accept any concept that runs contrary to the biblical model—period! Biblical fruit is always, under every circumstance, beneficial.

Apart from the biblical context, the word "good" means different things to different people and cultures. To some, good means making sure your kids have a designated driver when they go out drinking. To God, abstinence from drinking is good. He does not want anyone to stumble or to be required to accept unwarranted responsibility (1 Corinthians 10:31–32; 2 Corinthians 6:3). My mentor made it clear when she said, "I bet God hates the abuse you endure as His daughter more than He does divorce."

God describes Himself as "abounding in goodness" (Exodus 34:6, NKJV). The idea that we must be good in order to approach the throne is satan's devious scheme. His words seem just "good" enough to keep us from the very place of healing. Make sure your "good" is God's "good."

Choose your words carefully: if they are not based on God's Word and do not reflect His fruit, the enemy will use them to hinder souls.

My first marriage was one of these "wolves in sheep's clothing," one that I endured for way too long. However, one week after my divorce was final, after two decades of abuse, my God sent me a Kinsman Redeemer here on earth! He is Christ-like, humble, kind, pure, and good 1 Corinthians 13. He loves me, respects me, and brings me joy! He has helped me heal, resuscitated me from fear, loves my children, and, above all, God.

Romans 15:14 (NIV) says, "I myself am convinced, my brothers, that you yourselves are full of goodness, complete in knowledge and competent to instruct one another." Paul binds fruitfulness with full knowledge and a warning to serve each other. This gives us insight into what he knew and expected from Christians in Rome.

When we are hurting, it is most times a byproduct of evil done to us or by us. We can protect ourselves from evil with goodness. We can let God heal our evil hearts and allow forgiveness and goodness to master the pain. What unwanted consequences have come from the world's idea of goodness in your life?

Be aware that we are stepping into authority on this step. This is a bold step because God's authority will set things in alignment with His will. If we truly want to see others healed, we will use God's fruit to witness to others. We must empty ourselves out and allow God's love to flow in and through us. God calls us to hold others accountable at times, but most of the time, He does that silently as He works directly in their hearts. Our fruit, whether shown in righteous fervor, gentle admonition, or biblical authority, must first reside in love.

Bad Apples and Pomegranates

Many consequences come from satan's versions of God's fruit of the Spirit. We have seen much pain through the deception of worldly concepts of fruit. Let us look at the exact opposite of godly fruit and see what manifests from "bad apples." In our flesh, we exhibit bad fruit at times, and we just flat-out need to stop. Bad spiritual fruit is poisonous to the soul; its effects are more damaging to the soul than salmonella is to the body.

It may seem elementary and silly, but how often do you find yourself reacting in an ungodly manner? Well then, we need this little lesson on bad versus good. We are revisiting the antonym theory: the opposite of love is hate; the opposite of joy is rage; the opposite of peace is chaos; the opposite of patience is impatience; the opposite of kindness is meanness; the opposite of goodness is badness; the opposite of faithfulness is fearfulness; the opposite of gentleness is roughness; the opposite of self-control is self-indulgence.

When we are busy, rushing, and quick-tempered, when we justify our actions with excuses about having "too much to do," we are walking on either the wrong staircase or stepping without God.

The bad-apple mentality encourages us to retaliate. If we are attacked, we want to attack back. If we follow the devil's ways, we justify our retaliation. If God's fruit guides us, we keep our peace even when our flesh is screaming for us to slam someone verbally. Not only will the situation end on a better note, but every time we choose to react in peace, we gain ground in the fruit aisle of His love.

Guided by God's fruit, we attain a new sense of things. We are empowered to focus from our new, higher perspective in life. The fruit of God's Spirit resides inwardly in your every thought, word, and action. We have an endless supply of resources and tools in Him. God fills our lives with love, and this is the place where we gain ground and gather fruit. We are both healed and healing—all at once.

God abounds in fruitfulness and greatly desires to give us His fruit. We have degrees of faith as measured against this absolute standard. In the person who is converted but not healed, we see a pale reflection of this fruit. In the surrendered, vulnerable, healing, obedient person, we see a more vivid reflection. When we look in the mirror, we want to see a virtual cornucopia of fruit pouring out all over the place!

I remember when I bought my first pomegranate. I was well into my adult years and had gained some wisdom in Christ. I bought the pomegranate because I knew it was one of the seven foods listed in Deuteronomy 8:8. It is a beautiful fruit that adorned priestly garments. When I realized that it was full of flesh-covered seeds, I put three pomegranates in my shopping cart.

To my delight, when I cut into the fruit, a treasure trove of jewels poured out. The seeds were like beautiful prismatic rubies. The fruit was broken into chambers just like our hearts and full of red juice. I asked God to make my witness like that of a pomegranate. I asked for every seed that I put forth to be as beautiful as pomegranate seeds. I asked to pour out as much love as would fit. I asked that the red, red blood of Jesus would cover everyone who came near me.

Be a pomegranate for the Kingdom. If you still feel like a bad apple, ask God to anoint you with the harvest of a pomegranate. (Cool concept if the pomegranate was the fruit on the Tree of the Knowledge of Good and Evil in the Garden of Eden. I guess we can ask Him when we get there.)

We will make stepping up about something bigger now. We can position our lives to revolve around God as we move for the Kingdom, focusing on stretching our minds and spirits daily in a wholehearted task to understand, learn, and grow up in His Word. Now, we spend all our time in the courts of the temple, praising our Lord. We step up into fruit and a blessed and blessing life as we become consistent in our walk for Him.

Psalm 27:13–14 (NLT) says, "I am confident I will see the Lord's goodness while I am here in the land of the living. Wait patiently for the Lord. Be brave and courageous. Yes, wait patiently for the Lord."

Our steps gently trailed from sickness and hurt into healing. Our lives shifted as we grabbed hold of an intimate relationship with Him; now, we are allowing God to fill us up and bind us to Himself.

We placed our feet on the stairs of His expectation to bear much fruit. We journey now with balance as we are changing into His likeness. We are traveling with abundance and love. Our baskets are full. We will learn how to reside with these attributes, consistently making a place for God's wisdom.

Hallelujah, my beautiful climber, you are harvesting! You are giving, serving, and living for Christ so that He can return for His unblemished bride.

That is you!

Congratulations! You have done it again! You have successfully made it up another step: You have godly fruit for the journey! You have also added a new awareness to your day: you are serving.

Keep stepping. Step up into studying His Word.

Chapter Eleven

THE MASK OF CONSISTENCY

Step Eleven: God's Word Produces His Consistency

Appreciate your pastoral leaders who gave you the Word of God. Take a good look at the way they live, and let their faithfulness instruct you, as well as their truthfulness. There should be a consistency that runs through us all. For Jesus doesn't change—yesterday, today, tomorrow, He's always totally Himself.

Hebrews 13:7 (MSG)

When we are persistent in our approach to biblical standards, it is a sign that we have overcome our fleshly nature of inconsistency. At the same time, each step makes us godly in an area: "In word, in conversation, in charity, in spirit, in faith, or in purity" (1 Timothy 4:12, KJV); it is the cohesion that provides consecration into godliness. When we naturally live in His ways, we have stepped into His wisdom and become steady in His love.

We cannot build strong faith on weak understanding. When we feel tired and empty, let us go to His Word. To get to where He wants us to be, we will search for truth consistently, not just on the bad days.

When I was writing this book, there were days when all I felt like I was doing, aside from cleaning a toilet or two and tending to the family, was typing. I needed a break, and I needed some prayer, rejuvenation, and confirmation. But I had to be consistent regardless of my feelings; I had to finish the assignment.

We cannot remain constant in our fleshly state. In that condition, we most often repeat our bad choices and give up on the good ones. Godly consistency should run like a stream throughout our entire lives. Our plan is to mimic Christ with truthfulness and purity—and He is consistent, as we notice from our chapter verse, the Bible states, "Jesus Christ is the same yesterday and today and forever" (Hebrews 13:8, NIV).

We want to be consistent. We want to read, fast, listen, and pray consistently. We want to make sure what we do is not methodical but genuine from pure motives. God says that those with a clean heart will actually see Him (Matthew 5:8).

We know by now that our flesh will try to take over and tell us that this isn't a good time to read, seek Him, or fast. Excuses will pop up without effort. That is why we need the mind of Christ to rise up in us as a counterbalance to the lies. We want to be consistent to the cross.

Consistent Godly Stepping

Consistency is a major player on the stairs to healing. It is the upward rhythm or motion that we keep. Steadfastness is so intricate a part of the duration and endurance of our success that, without its influence, we will fail. We see excellence when we see Godly consistency in our behavior.

Three chapters a day keeps the devil away!

We are consistent when we are obeying the Spirit and the Word. I have realized, walking through "the temple," that, more than anything, my consistency to God's ways is what ensures the longevity of my healed state. All the steps prior are important and necessary. This step is the center step of the impartation stairs; it is the glue that binds them all. We have to step out all our principles and actions consistently day by day, hour by hour, minute by minute, unto perfection. We cannot deviate or let up.

Just like our awareness of hope, faith, praying, reading, worshiping, resting, fasting, listening, giving, and serving, studying has got to be done consistently to be of use. It is His daily bread. We are a give-up society. We stick with things until we get bored or tired or until something new comes along.

Do not let the enemy determine your outcomes by allowing him to feed you lies.

"He was a murderer from the beginning. He has always hated the truth, because there is no truth in him. When he lies, it is consistent with his character; for he is a liar and the father of lies" (John 8:44, NLT).

When I read this scripture, it makes me want to never turn and walk back down. By nature, we are flighty and shifty. We do not need anybody's help to quit. What we need is to stand on the Rock consistently. Jesus stays the same always; all else is sinking sand.

Remain consistent, even when the road gets tougher. Do you ever wonder why some people seem to get the easy road? Does your road always seem to be on the edge of a ridge of falling rocks? Do your stairs seem steeper than other people's?

When I go for a run, I pick a starting point and a stopping point. Then, I choose consistency with no option of stopping. I want to remain victorious. But the route is often grueling, and I ask Him why.

One day, I cried out, "Why, Jesus?" He answered me at the very end of a long and trying path.

"You would not appreciate it otherwise. You would not be satisfied if your work was not grueling." His answer was ironic because I thought I was trying to combat frustration (the opposite of satisfaction) with my run. He told me not to question His techniques in my life because *I Am* the one who determines them.

As I puzzled through His words, He asked me to look back over my life and tell Him what I loved the most and what mattered most to me. As I glanced back into my past, I began to weep. The things that hurt the most meant the most to me. He told me some of His saints were completely content with the simple, easy road. He told me I was the exact opposite; therefore, I had to have a challenge.

He said that even in the physical, I expressed this. When I ran, I made sure it was a marathon. I couldn't just be part of the class; I had to teach it. My passions were extreme, and my obedience was insane. My trials were not middle of the road but hanging off a cliff. He was making me adhere to how He had made me and how He sees pleasure in me.

When I divorced, it was the worst experience ever. When I was totally beaten down prior to the divorce, I experienced a dark night of the soul. When I felt fear, I felt it to its highest intensity. I would ask God why. Why my children? Why my marriage? Why do I feel like you are gone? Please help!

He asked me why I would question Him when it was He who created me. He wanted to know why everything had to be right now when all He wanted to do was give me the ability to handle the blessings first. He told me I was the one who chose the pain. He reminded me of my free will, and He walked me back and showed me the forks in the road that I did not take.

I did not stop running as I wept and screamed at the top of my lungs, "I love You, Jesus, with everything in me! I thank You for making me so extreme because while the bad may be really bad, the good I pray will someday purely and remarkably glorify You. Your will for me is incredible. And, yes, You know me and love me, and regardless of the pain, I will press towards the goal in You."

I screamed these words as I sweated in the noonday sun. I refused to stop running regardless of exhaustion until I came to the predetermined stopping point. Now, you can take this story and begin running, or you can realize that your consistency determines your destiny. When we have faith that God is in control, all we have to do is walk out His plan.

God's plan for you is perfect and in perfect order. If something is not part of His plan, we should reject it, too. God knows you better than you can ever know yourself. Trusting consistently that He has your life taken care of is enough. He has not left a single detail to chance. As long as you have breath, breathe for Him; He is listening and guiding your steps. They will be good steps.

Twenty-Six Point Two

Godly consistency only comes through the cross of Christ. We can attain productive, purpose-driven consistency only through diligence toward God's call. To know the power of victory, you must cross the finish line. First, however, you must train your body, mind, and heart to run the race with a victorious mindset.

Speaking of running, I ran the Chicago Marathon. Running 26.2 miles is tough. It takes never giving up and never stopping to turn around to look back. It may sound like a diversion, but running is a gift the Lord has given me. I feel God's pleasure when I run. What are the talents God has blessed in you? How consistently do you use them? What have they taught you?

Running gets you places fast, but you must be careful not to get ahead of God. When I am injured, I see how He gently slows me down and sometimes stops me to rest in Him and heal. My running has taught me a lot about endurance in trials and obedience in finishing the things I start.

More than anything, it has taught me about consistency. Without steady training, you lose your endurance and capability. Without consistent pacing, you lose your time and placement. Both are imperative to fulfilling our God-ordained purpose, preparation, and position. Without a consistent mindset of finishing the race, you will lose—period.

Running has taught me to trust Him when I feel like running back down all the steps that I have fought so hard to climb. It has taught me to push forward when I feel pain and want to give up more than anything. It has taught me that without consistent and proper training, there is no way to succeed. All these lessons are very important on this step.

We are winning the greatest victory when we feel the most opposition and are the most tempted to turn around or stop. We cannot always see the blessing, but we will be prepared and have faith that God has greatness in store for us. If we could see it, there would be no need for faith.

When the race gets the best of you, stand still if that is all you can do. But my advice is, be consistent in the promise of His Word and pray. Do not give up; stay in the blood. Fight the good fight of faith. We do not like to be uncomfortable; however, that is the very place we must visit right before we reach the place of peace, blessing, and glory.

Throughout the Chicago Marathon, I said Jesus' name through sweat and breathlessness. I prayed through the entire last half of that race. I had no big plans. In fact, my only plan was to track with the eight-minute mile marker sign. I whispered the name of Jesus in order to stay consistent with my pace up the hills. I said it when I felt like there was nothing more in me. I allowed Him to move for me when the marker sign got too far ahead in the distance. When I hurt, I gave Him the pain.

I finished that race in three hours and forty minutes flat, chip time. That was the cut-off for qualifying for the Boston Marathon. I am not telling you this for your kudos. I am sharing this because I did not even know I could qualify or what qualifying was all about. Sound familiar to my room in "Damascus"? However, God saw my heart and my persistence, and He blessed me. All glory and honor go to Him in our undertakings.

I had accomplished two things with my Savior, one of which I had not the sense to even plan for. My Jesus always says, "If we are merely faithful, Jesus trumps our every request."

Are you making glorious plans with your talents? Make sure you are not selling yourself short. Do you know that with God, anything is possible?

Majestic Trailer Park

Growing up, as you know, I had a general lack of godly consistency. However, there was hope for me through both sets of grandparents, especially my father's parents, because of their proximity. I spent a lot of time with them. The time was so precious that it was magnified in my thinking. Their steadiness to each other and me resides at the top of my memory bank.

Nonnie would always tell me, "Little girls are supposed to be made of sugar, spice, and everything nice."

When I was a little girl, I did not feel like that. I liked sugar and spice; it was an endearing way of describing my personality, but the "everything nice" part bothered me. I felt lonely and broken and did not feel like everything or anything, especially something nice.

My nonnie and grandpa loved to give me little sayings and sing to me. Nonnie would play the piano with her graceful fingers; she would play "Maria" from *The Sound of Music*, and we would sing it together. Then, Nonnie and Grandpa would tell me that they loved me. We sang all the time in my grandparents' trailer in south Texas, near the border of Mexico. They could not have had a mansion that would have made me happier.

The trailer park was like an adventure park. It had a shuffleboard, a pool, and cool things in everyone's front yard. The streets resembled a flea market. There were things spinning, sparkling, and waving. There were gnomes, flamingos, fountains, and flags. Some trailers were even decorated for Christmas all year long. They either forgot or were practical and left the stuff up for the next year. What I remember most in the midst of all of this was that Grandpa loved Nonnie, Nonnie loved Grandpa, and they provided a pure, safe, stable place in my life.

We would wake up at the same time every morning and eat a big, nourishing breakfast. Later, we had lunch, followed by dinner. In between, we had yard work, backgammon, and lots of love. Consistency and calm were the hallmarks of that majestic trailer park. The glue in my grandparents' relationship would be the thing I looked for when Jesus came calling. Consistency for the fight out of the wrong union, but I knew exactly what to look for when I met Sam. It gave me something to attain to. What good can you mimic from life (even if it only happened once)?

Nonnie's name was Vera, so I always thought it was neat that she had an aloe vera plant out behind the trailer. When I would fall off my bike, she would walk out back, hack off a huge chunk of the plant, and rub the green ooze on my injury, regardless of the size of the wound. Nonnie was always loving, kind, sober, vigilant, and working—as was Grandpa.

Out by the aloe vera plant was Nonnie's fountain with a statue of a little girl in the middle. Nonnie used to say, "That is you."

She had three boys. I think I blessed her as much as she blessed me. Finally, in her old age, and with much wisdom and time to share, God allowed her a little girl. I loved her and my grandpa so much. I felt safe and knew love when I was with them.

I remember how I loved wearing Nonnie's square dancing costumes when I was eight. My favorite quest was to rifle through her jewelry box. Then, I would load myself up with big, sparkly rhinestones that conveniently clipped to almost anything, including my ears. This dress-up was practice for my reign as Maskquerade Queen. As an innocent child, I felt just like a mask remover, with the good King and the good Queen in the trailer in south Texas.

Nonnie knew of my passion for royalty. She needed her square dancing clothes but did not want to send me home without proper my queen's ball protocol. Therefore, she would spend hours sewing formal, ruffled dresses. My favorite attire for every occasion was a royal garment.

I wore these long dresses the way other kids wore shorts and T-shirts. My bicycle spokes always seemed to grab the lace and ring the bell sewn into the hem. I sported ankle-length gowns, whether playing in the woods, riding my bike, or strolling down the street. I insisted the bells be sewn into the hems with velvet bows. I could not just look like a mask remover; I wanted to be accompanied by a royal chime—a royal jingle, so to speak. I knew all the way back then that it was not enough just to look the part; you had to smell the part, be the part, and sound the part as well. When I wanted something, I wanted it engrained in me; every fiber counted.

Nonnie and Grandpa, a.k.a. Birdie and the Colonel, were beacons of consistency that I would remember all my my life. Looking back, I can see that the little things...the hidden things...matter most. The way we act day in and day out is what adds up to significance (Zechariah 4:10).

"Maria," the song Nonnie used to sing with me, was no accident. I noticed, even at such a young age and unchurched as I was, the line: "Her penitence was real." The words stuck with me. I came back to them years later. God sees your heart. He knows its condition. Let us not forget that daily humility and penitence take us before the throne of God.

Symbols of the Supernatural

As I have mentioned before, God often shows us in the natural realm what He is performing in the supernatural. He is faithfully consistent in this. We are like little girls standing on their fathers' feet; He sees our smiles as we dance with Him. He takes pleasure in the consistency He sees developing in us. We are mask removers.

I attempted to capture a certain feeling with the title of this book and the importance of always knowing that satan is going to attempt to derail us into his maskquerade for he and his angels maskquerade as angels of light. Don't ever think you've got it licked; you gain awareness, and he steps up his deception. Be wise and keep humble; always be willing to remove a mask or two.

Think back to when you first saw God. Stop everything and move the wind just for you. That moment reveals what being a child of the Most High means. He will stop everything for you and replace your old with new.

I remember when I met Him, that moment when I finally decided to die out. I could feel the velvet silkiness of the royal garment as He placed it over my weak shoulders. He had adorned the edges with pomegranates, awareness, and tassels. The garment produced sounds like the gowns Nonnie used to make me, but instead of the peal of a small bell, it was the shimmering harmony of chimes. My ears heard deep and high pitches. The resonance produced the same melody that the angels hummed. My nose drew in the aromatic smell of raw silk and linen all in one breath; it was a deep, earthy, living scent that traveled straight into the soul.

My new mantle was not heavy, hot, or scratchy; the adornment was perfect. I was finally clothed like proper royalty, the cloak of freedom, joy, and peace. I looked down, and my sash read, "Forgiven, for her penitence is real." The salt from my tears ran into my mouth as I spoke, "Jesus, King of kings and Lord of lords, there is nothing that You do not control, and my heart is Yours forever."

Let Him place a new mantle on you. If you feel like your consistency in healing has been difficult, allow Him to give you His burden and yoke

(Matthew 11:28). This time, it will not just be a costume to hide the pain. Your new freedom in Christ will be authority to reign over your pain.

Our Lord desires to adorn us in His best, changing every fiber, opening our eyes and ears to hear, and encasing us with the scent of heaven. He stands waiting to amend our garments, crown us in beauty, and restore our joy:

[He has sent Me to]...provide for those who grieve in Zion—to bestow on them a crown of beauty instead of ashes, the oil of gladness instead of mourning, and a garment of praise instead of a spirit of despair.

Isaiah 61:3 (NIV)

The Rhythm of His Word

When we are consistent in our studies, we allow wisdom to settle in on us, and we discover the blessing of purpose uncovered by our healing.

Studying is the awareness we are going to add on this stair. We must not only read the Word of God but also study it diligently. It is not just for pastors or clergy. Learning God's Word is for us. The study should be our daily bread for life. When we truly study, we assimilate God's methods and take up His power for ourselves.

Finding the meaning in each word that God has linked together in rhythm and synchronicity produces life. I told the women in my accountability group one night that I would not be the least bit shocked if my Bible began to beat or pulse just like a heart. His Word is alive, and every word has unending depth; every page pumps life into our being.

When we study, we rightly divide the Word and join the Word together. When God leads you to a particular verse, connect it to the one above and the one below. See how the message fits in contextually within the chapter and book. Find out who wrote it and to whom it was written, and learn where, when, and why it was written. Then, prayerfully take the Scripture and see where else in the Bible you see the same theme, the same meaning, or the same choice of words.

God's Word is not like any other book; it is alive. Did you hear me? The Bible is alive. The actual words are full of life-giving power. They heal, deliver, warn, rebuke, guide, protect, comfort, love...I promise this is truth. All you need to experience this truth is faith and salvation. Then, the baptism of the Spirit helps the deeper revelation:

> *For the word of God is living and active. Sharper than any double-edged sword, it penetrates even to dividing soul and spirit, joints and marrow; it judges the thoughts and attitudes of the heart.*
>
> Hebrews 4:12 (NIV)

Are you getting this? I believe you are! You are doing so well that we are going to press further with God by asking Him to impart wisdom into our healing life. Wisdom is what will further bind us to His hem, the only royal garment we need. He is waiting for you to ask for His gifts, His wisdom, and more faith to assist you in your healthy life.

Congratulations, you have successfully made it up another step: You are consistent in Godly stepping. You have also added another awareness: you are studying God's Word on your journey. We only have two more stairs to climb. Keep stepping!

Chapter Twelve

WISDOM: THE UNVEILING

Step Twelve: Functioning in Your Purpose is Wise

Get wisdom, get understanding; do not forget my words or swerve from them. Do not forsake wisdom, and she will protect you; love her, and she will watch over you. Wisdom is supreme; therefore get wisdom. Though it cost all you have, get understanding. Esteem her, and she will exalt you; embrace her, and she will honor you. She will set a garland of grace on your head and present you with a crown of splendor.

Proverbs 4:5–9 (NIV)

Wisdom is what occurs when we allow God to transform our minds as He intends, broaden the understanding of our hearts, and widen our capacity to contain His glory. Wisdom is the seed of revelation and the blossom of healing. Wise steps are peaceful, joyful steps. Wisdom is represented as a woman in Scripture; she is beautiful, and we are becoming her. She is also "proved right by her actions" (Matthew 11:19). So, let's prove her right in our healing.

I see wisdom when I see someone covered in peace and letting God fight for them in a time of trial. Wisdom is love and stillness when the flesh says to struggle. Wisdom resides inside of faith, love, peace, joy, goodness, faithfulness, patience, kindness, gentleness, and self–control. Wisdom is joy in the midst of pain and loving forgiveness when we want to hate. The wisest people are willing to give their wealth away in exchange for wisdom.

Knowledge is fact, information, and data; it is what you gain from education. Wisdom is the key to purpose. It unlocks knowledge and helps us to utilize it effectively. If consistency causes us to ascend the steps in a fluid motion, wisdom enables us to discern the perfect pace and flow in the current of love that keeps the motion going. True wisdom, godly wisdom can only be grasped through access to the Spirit of God and His Word.

First Corinthians 2:9–10 says:

> *However, as it is written: "No eye has seen, no ear has heard, no mind has conceived what God has prepared for those who love Him"—but God has revealed it to us by his Spirit. The Spirit searches all things, even the deep things of God.*
>
> 1 Corinthians 2:9–10 (NIV)

We have taken this passage out of a chapter on spiritual wisdom. Paul concludes the chapter by telling us, "We have the mind of Christ" (1 Corinthians 2:16, NIV).

Are you allowing God to change your mind with His wisdom? Are you allowing Him to transfer all of His love into your heart? If you are willing, ask Him; He is more than willing to fulfill your request.

When we are transformed by Him, we can better walk in purity and humility. Remember that our initial steps into healing were meant to clean us out. These latter steps are meant to keep us healthy; they change us by teaching us to rely on and receive from Him. We, in turn, are filled with His glory.

I went to seminary. God put me there for more than just knowledge. I love studying Scripture. Knowing all of Paul's missionary journeys, all the dates, all the prophets from Genesis up, and all the history gives me more information. Knowing all the power behind those journeys, understanding the symbolism in the dates, and hearing the hearts of the prophets for then and today gives me wisdom about the scriptures.

I was full of knowledge well into my healing, even revelation, but it was not until I suffered, and suffered, and suffered, and suffered some more, and obeyed what did not make sense to me or what I did not want to endure like Jesus, "Please take this cup," moments that it became the living waters of wisdom. The jump off the cliff into an abyss type of sacrifice for others and Christ is where our greatest transformations occur.

This encounter activates knowledge into authority. I became a healing and healed vessel to heal for God. Such supernatural occurrences cannot be explained with words; you have to experience them by walking with faith through life's trials and count them all as joy.

God's Fivefold Plan

Now that I have your trust, I want to tell you that the fivefold ministry, as well as the gifts, miracles, signs, dreams, visions, and wonders, are for today. We are about to cover some of these in this chapter, and I pray that you glean true wisdom from our study. Let me share my encounter with a true prophet; not one that just has the gift of prophecy (which we are about to study) but an ordained officer.

First, let me briefly explain prophecy. Revelation 19:10 (KJV) tells us, "Worship God! For the testimony of Jesus is the spirit of prophecy." Jesus' testimony is life and life abundant. It is the actual healing we have experienced. We make things too complicated. Prophecy is God's love for us manifested in His power through His saints.

Once again, I was not sure what I was about to experience, but like a little girl, I walked eyes wide open and my heart into God's arms through a ministry I had never experienced before. Boxing God up in our thinking by deciding to cease or ignore things we cannot rationalize or have not yet experienced in His Word holds us in bondage. Prophets are here, and they are very real.

Anyone who receives a prophet because he is a prophet will receive a prophet's reward, and anyone who receives a righteous man because he is a righteous man will receive a righteous man's reward (Matthew 10:41).

I stepped into a prayer room with a friend, and after we had spent some time in the presence of God, allowing Him to flow into the depths of our souls, further healing us for purity in our purpose, blood came gushing out of my nose. When it finally stopped, I walked out of that room, a changed vessel for God. What happened? I don't know. All I know is that a demand for change occurred. The change took several years, and I'm still changing today, so don't think this is a quick fix, overnight thing.

Remember that God uses physical signs to disclose and represent spiritual events. My spiritual blood transfusion activated the natural gifts and called on my life with supernatural power infused with the love of God to glorify His Kingdom.

This gift is proven true in Scripture and in my life experience. I want these encounters to be commonplace among you; they are healing, gifts, and call-activating opportunities. I did not just walk in, fall out and bleed. I worked hard. I let a lot of my flesh die out and stood with only faith at times for the reward.

In fact, that experience birthed me into the true understanding of prophecy. I was suddenly captivated by a larger dose of His love and, this time, a new level of His glory.

This advancement into His ways allowed for more deep revelation in my life. When I was barely out of treatment years earlier, I had a dream, but it wasn't until wisdom arrived at this step that it was interpreted: Sam and I were at the beach in a contemporary house with a convertible car parked in the garage, which is not our taste. This showed me that this is His ministry, not ours. My husband, Sam, was jogging, telling me he was healthy in our old age. I was on the balcony looking out over a strangely calm yet raging sea. I felt peace as the moon filled the sky, although it was daytime and the moon was covered in blood.

I did not even know that there was Scripture describing this scene minus the "Brady bunch house" until this period of my life years later (Luke 21:25 and Acts 2:20). Signs and wonders are here and coming in abundance for us and the next generation. We need to be healthy enough to raise them up in the Word. Study, find wisdom, and stand in your purpose in order to impart power to our children and grandchildren, knowing how to walk them into their call.

Some of the most intelligent Bible scholars will never advance in the ability to instruct in power if they refuse to walk the stairs, stepping out of their head knowledge and into His wisdom. Once you have had an experience, you are no longer at the mercy of an argument. We will now pass the step of knowledge and begin to study wisdom to flow in our purpose for His Kingdom to come.

Explanations regarding wisdom can be perplexing; wisdom is one of those things we understand after it is established in our lives. Just as hope transforms into faith, obedience and knowledge flow into wisdom (when we let the Holy Spirit lead us).

You will know wisdom's power the minute God's perception is born in you. Wisdom is God's, and only God can impart the power to see beyond our limited minds in our spirit. He said it is with wisdom that He formed the earth (Jeremiah 10:12).

The Purpose of Wisdom

First, we need to recognize what pulls wisdom in and what lets wisdom out. Proverbs 2:10 tells us it is our heart that is the entry of wisdom. When we make the shift to accept and release only God's truths from our heart, we are flowing in His wisdom. The whole world sought audience with Solomon to hear the wisdom God had put in his heart (1 Kings 10:24).

You are aware by now that I write and study a lot. Right before God's prophet took me in, I had to release all ownership of my intellect. Let me explain. I had filled my computer with exegesis papers, notes, Bible studies, this book, a guided journal, and so on. I would spend hours reading, writing Bible studies, and then saving them to protect my "important" knowledge. I would take days out to prepare notes for speaking engagements, all while God was waiting on me to let Him be my source.

I came home one day excited to begin another "deep" Bible study. When I turned on my computer, there was nothing but a blue screen. I guess it was better than having my hip out of joint. I left my knowledge and information at the foot of the cross while kicking, screaming, and trying to resurrect my hard drive in government "clean rooms" with men in beekeeper suits.

There I was, crying on the floor, surrounded in the refuse of my lost identity. I did not realize that, in the midst of my broken crowns and ripped sashes, He could best use me. He lovingly whispered about how Solomon's temple was glorious to Him, but because even a speck of evil had entered, He had to take it down. He told me He only destroys to restore unto glory; He said that if I trusted Him, He would put wisdom in my heart that no person could teach me and no person or event could take from me.

When I submitted to His love above all else and walked humbly through that prayer room, bloody nose and all, I became His hard drive, and the hard drive of my flesh was gone. He activated and deepened my spirit to contain more of Him and His love. Now, I spend only what He requires preparing to speak because I only want it to be Him speaking through me forever.

Most of us have devoted much time to study, and I thank the Lord for it. It has paved the way for amazing advancements and all kinds of wonderful inventions. However, as far as saving souls and bringing spiritual healing, our soul knowledge is useless if not coupled with His Spirit's wisdom.

The minute I digested the Books of 1 and 2 Kings and learned about David's life, I realized that as long as our hearts are truly repentant and we realize our need for Him, our faith stream continues, and God hears us. However, do we hear Him back? This is how faith enters, so we need to be careful to listen.

Even in sin, David was in the lineage of the king of wisdom. David's son, Solomon, would crave the very heart of God's wise counsel. God saw Solomon's heart and answered his plea. The humility and purity of letting nothing come between us and God keeps us healthy. Even Solomon fell away toward the end. We do not want to heal and then step back.

Wisdom comes from one source: God. You obtain wisdom when you ask for the entire revelation of Christ and the Word of God—precept upon precept, nothing added, nothing taken away—to be sewn into your heart. Problems arise when we seek wisdom in the wrong places and fall prey to false doctrine.

The Fear of the Lord

We are all in search of something God quietly tucked away in the Book of Job. It is beautiful and descriptive, and it takes you on a journey into the depths of the earth and through the secret trails that we know not. I have felt like Job and have lived like him, too, and what it gave me was a reverential fear to always stay in God's will. He sums it up by saying, "The fear of the Lord—that is wisdom, and to shun evil is understanding" (Job 28:28, NIV).

People often live in the shelter of their own might, never to feel the torrent of wind from an eagle's wing (see Isaiah 40:31). For instance, we need to teach and allow the gifts that the churches are to operate and let them flow. God is not always tangible. He is amazing. Our imposition of practicality on spirituality is satan's way of making sure revival does not break out. Let us allow God to clothe us in the majestic royalty He intended so that countless generations can be blessed.

We are going to learn about our giftings so that we can function in our purpose. Our life application or action for the step of wisdom is functioning in our purpose or knowing and owning our purpose in Christ. I am going to address the administration gifts only by title, for they are self-explanatory. I will give examples and some explanation of the spiritual gifts because they are the exact thing I am talking about here. We will also cover the importance of the fivefold ministry.

The very fact that so many avoid God's spiritual gifts, entirely or in part, is the exact proof of their power. People do not flinch when it comes to accepting the administrative gifting, but the intangible, spiritual gifts—that is another story.

When I began receiving wisdom, I found that God impressed the knowledge of His spiritual gifts on me steadily by actual examples in my ministry. I feel like they were a part of the heart of wisdom. Our faith grows when we conceive and believe a prophecy and then actually see it birthed. God's spiritual gifts are this exact thing conceptually. They are a belief in the supernatural and, when they touch the natural, our faith grows. Wisdom's seed is first in faith.

God's purpose for us is to faithfully find and then function in our purpose in Him with wisdom. God has healed you. He has brought you out of the mire and into His temple. He has given you His Spirit and His Word for your journey. First Corinthians 1:7–8 says:

Therefore you do not lack any spiritual gift as you eagerly wait for our Lord Jesus Christ to be revealed. He will keep you strong to the end, so that you will be blameless on the day of our Lord Jesus Christ.

1 Corinthians 1:7–8

We can operate at times in all of the gifts, but we will have certain gifts that are stronger. This helps to reveal our function to strengthen the Body and affirms our call. This study will be brief because you need to begin to experience these things to fully understand them. We will gain knowledge on the gifts and then you can go to God to ask for the activation of them unto wisdom.

God tells us to pursue the gifts. Have you asked for specific gifts for your life? Our godly actions done in the humility that stems from wisdom will guide us to our gifts. The first gifts we will briefly cover are the gifts of administration (no irony that the first gift listed is a spiritual gift). First, let's touch on what I call "a big lump of gifts in Romans" for the fact that many seem randomly pressed together here. They are found in Romans 12:6–8:

We have different gifts, according to the grace given us. If a man's gift is prophesying, let him use it in proportion to his faith. If it is serving, let him serve; if it is teaching, let him teach; if it is encouraging, let him encourage; if it is contributing to the needs of others, let him give generously; if it is leadership, let him govern diligently; if it is showing mercy, let him do it cheerfully.

Romans 12:6–8 (NIV)

By the way, the next chapter, Romans 13, describes our debt to love others (Romans 13:8). Unless gifts operate from the heart of love, they will be ineffective at best and dangerous at worst.

Leadership ministry gifts are described in Ephesians 4:11 (NIV): "It was He who gave some to be apostles, some to be prophets, some to be evangelists, and some to be pastors and teachers." You can use your five fingers to remember these. This is the fivefold ministry and is the backbone of the Church, with Christ as its Head. The foundation is the prophets and apostles (Ephesians 2:20–22). Many churches today are hurting because they do not accept this foundation.

First Corinthians 12 is a great chapter to study. This letter describes the spiritual gifts and breaks down some administrative gifts as well. Once again, love is the chapter that follows this dissertation. In fact, this book ends its last step in love.

I want to touch on the gifts of the Spirit because they are exactly that: gifts. They are beautiful, and we need to pursue them. They admonish, bring revelation, edify, strengthen, encourage, and teach us. The nine spiritual gifts divide into three sections, each housing three gifts.

During my studies, I learned that the nine could be neatly broken down in these three categories, each with three sub-categories. They are the revelation gifts (word of wisdom, word of knowledge, discerning of spirits), the power gifts (gift of faith, gift of healing, working of miracles), and the gifts of inspiration (prophecy, tongues, the interpretation of tongues) (1 Corinthians 12).

We must first have the Spirit in us in order to tap into His spiritual gifts. The Bible states that we are all eligible until the end (1 Corinthians 13:10), and the end has not arrived yet. Several gifts that are alive and active today are merged into the following scriptures: Matthew 28:18–20 and Mark 16:15–18). They are sandwiched in with The Great Commission, which we can handle. The things we cannot explain in a natural way are that some seemingly want to omit or cease. Why, I do not know, as it is power for our dying lives.

In addition to not denying any part of Scripture, we need to be cautious of blind guides who will try to squelch our gifts. God talks about them in the Seven Woes to the church in Matthew 23. People have been denying, abusing, and falsifying the gifts. In turn, this has done a great disservice to people's faith. Encourage one another with the authenticity that comes only through God's Holy Spirit. Remember that the very purpose of the gifts is to heal, edify, warn, and reveal.

If you are confused about the gifts, ask God to show you. Remember, He is no respecter of persons. Why would He extend the gifts to me and not to you? You are the Church; if you allow Him, God will keep you clean of man's ideologies so that His power is not stagnated by misguided resistance. He can keep us Kingdom-minded, opinion-free, producing fruit, healing, healing others, and saving souls.

When we like to reside in God's Spirit and prefer His Spirit to reside in us, we are wise. This is glory. My witness today of His Spirit performing real-life miracles, healings, and infillings (with all the gifts in operation) leads me to a definitive conclusion: there has been no cessation of God's gifts, nor does He intend one.

Let us look at an example from my life of the gifts in action. When God filled me with the Holy Spirit, my mentor spoke in an unknown prayer language. When she spoke in English during the revelation, she said things that only God and I knew about. The word of knowledge was in operation.

My healing and the transforming of my knowledge into wisdom were manifestations of the power gifts that were given to me through a vessel or directly from the Holy Spirit. Many may mock, but I say, "Do not grieve the Holy Spirit. Do not deride that which is truth. He holds the lightning and the thunder."

I have evidence of tongues from my infilling (Acts 2:4; 19:6). This is different from the gifts of inspiration for the Church. This private prayer language allows me to go unhindered to the throne room, strengthens our spirit, and helps us to receive deeper revelation.

In the same way, the Spirit helps us in our weakness. We do not know what we ought to pray for, but the Spirit Himself intercedes for us with groans that words cannot express (Romans 8:26).

If you are infilled with God's Holy Spirit, you have access to this also. If it did not overcome you upon transformation, ask for it. I had to. Acts 1:8 (KJV) says, "Ye shall receive power, after that the Holy Ghost is come upon you."

If you really want to stay healed and want to see God, then seek God on every level. If we oppress these gifts or say they have ceased, we subject ourselves to lesser blessings. Why would God cease healings of any kind? We must not ignore or fear the obvious. We must let God speak to us and let Him anoint us with His gifts.

We read Acts; we study Acts; we live Acts. If satan can keep us fearful or ignorant, then he succeeds against us; if he can accomplish all of this inside the Church, he can enforce endless cycles of sickness.

Oh, Peter, You Didn't

Psalm 138:8 (CSB) says: "The Lord will fulfill [His purpose] for me; Your love, O Lord, endures forever—do not abandon the works of Your hands."

His love, mercy, and grace are without end. Do you remember the fateful exchange between Peter and Jesus the night before He died? "Jesus answered, 'Die for Me? I tell you the truth, Peter—before the rooster crows tomorrow morning, you will deny three times that you even know Me" (John 13:38, NLT).

Peter did, in fact, deny Jesus three times. Yet, Jesus went on to give him not only the keys of the Kingdom (Matthew 16:19) but also asked him to shepherd and feed His flock (John 21:15–17). Jesus gave Peter purpose after his sin and asked him to combat his denial with love. In asking Peter three times whether he loved Jesus, the Lord requested one life-giving statement for each act of denial.

God shows us here that there is no sin too big for Him to cover in love. He gives us a purpose once we shed the walls of the devil's maskquerade of denial. He gives us a ministry so that we will stand up and say, "Thou art the Christ," as Peter did in Mark 8:29 (KJV).

A wise saint once told me to pray that God would increase my capacity in order to hold more of His wisdom. His knowledge is without end. His wisdom is infinite. His understanding cannot be fully captured and cannot be exhausted. Just as we are praying for wisdom, we will pray for our Godly purpose to surface. We will pray for God to reveal our giftings and bestow His spiritual gifts on us.

Isaiah 11:1–2 made an irrevocable promise, one that I have mentioned in a different light previously, showing the beautiful depth and multitude of ways Scripture can be used:

Out of the stump of David's family will grow a shoot—yes, a new Branch bearing fruit from the old root. And the Spirit of the Lord will rest on Him—the Spirit of wisdom and understanding, the Spirit of counsel and might, the Spirit of knowledge and the fear of the Lord.

Isaiah 11:1–2 (NLT)

You are grafted into that new fruit-bearing branch. You have allowed the Spirit of power to remain in you, and you are healthy because of Him. We need to ask for more of Him and for more room to contain all of Him. Just as our fruit basket is overflowing, and we need to balance it as we step up, we also need wisdom and the current of love to be so strong and full that upward is the only possible direction we can take. Our gifts and our studies provide proof of our healing, just as our giving and serving take us into the flow of our God-ordained purpose.

We have hope and faith for every step. We are praying, reading, worshiping, resting, fasting, listening, giving, serving, and studying—all with a purpose in Christ. In our pursuit of God, love trumps all. Everything ends in love. We pray that He shows us and gives us His love to live in and to give out. Our healing is in direct proportion to the amount of God's love we will allow to flow through us.

If any of you lacks wisdom, he should ask God, who gives generously to all without finding fault, and it will be given to him. But when he asks, he must believe and not doubt (James 1:5–6).

Who is wise and understanding among you? Let him show it by his good life, by deeds done in the humility that comes from wisdom (James 3:13).

Congratulations! You have stepped into wisdom. You understand His purpose and gifts for your journey. There is only one more stair left to climb. The last one is the best one yet! Beautiful sister, keep stepping. Step up into His love!

Chapter Thirteen

THE TOPOGRAPHY OF GOD'S LOVE

Step Thirteen: God's Love in Everything

"The most important one," answered Jesus, "is this: 'Hear, O Israel, the Lord our God, the Lord is one. Love the Lord your God with all your heart and with all your soul and with all your mind and with all your strength.' The second is this: 'Love your neighbor as yourself.' There is no commandment greater than these."

Mark 12:29–31 (NIV)

When we allow the love of God, through the acceptance of Christ and the fullness of His Holy Spirit, to permeate every cell of our unworthy being, we begin to emit His love to others. We are now not only healed and healing vessels; we are healers as well. God's love in us is the all-encompassing reason for our consistent upward motion and an important determining factor in the direction those around us take. To share His unceasing love is the mightiest purpose of all.

As we trust our experience with the steps, let us grasp the handrail, turn and look back just for a moment, and see how far we have come. Looking back, we will always remember our pain in order to operate with humility, grace, and mercy, but we will not reside in the pain of our dark days in the maskquerade. Your pain is now your testimony!

It is not by our might that we stand this far up; our triumph is only by His Spirit (Zechariah 4:6). This is God's stairway built by His grace. There is nothing we did, no obedience so great or prayer so profound as to deserve even the deadbolt to have been unlatched. We step up firmly into God's love with a surrendered heart filled with only purity and humility.

I am so proud of you for persevering. I am so thankful that you are yet another unmasked person added to the ranks of the healed and healing. We are a Kingdom of mighty mask removers vying for a cause much greater than our sickness. We now have a testimony to share, a history of stepping in power and love with Christ.

Philemon 1:6 (NIV) describes our goal: "I pray that you may be active in sharing your faith, so that you will have a full understanding of every good thing we have in Christ."

Looking back on the tiny, now insignificant door of sickness and shame, I realize that the very moment I knew I wanted out of the darkness was the moment that I let go of everything. I released everything I thought I loved and everything I did love. Look back for a moment. Do you see the same response? The devil no longer has you trapped!

God tells us that everything comes down to love. I released not only my pain but also my first husband, marriage, daughters, son, mother, father, family, hopes, dreams, freedom, friends, finances, choices, gifts, purpose, life, everything—even my hard drive. We give up all we love. We give it all to Him. We do not know for sure whether we will get any of it back or if we even want particular parts back. That is the hardest part.

When we gave it up, He took what was not love and removed it like a vapor. He showed us the difference between love and lust, pain and healing, fear and faith, death and life. He then began to reestablish those things that were of His love back into our lives. We see Him adding love where we never expected to find it. We see the impossible becoming possible only by His love.

The famous thirteenth chapter of 1 Corinthians has real meaning to us now:

Love is patient, love is kind. It does not envy, it does not boast, it is not proud. It is not rude, it is not self-seeking, it is not easily angered, it keeps no record of wrongs. Love does not delight in evil but rejoices with the truth. It always protects, always trusts, always hopes, always perseveres.

Love never fails. But where there are prophecies, they will cease; where there are tongues, they will be stilled; where there is knowledge, it will pass away.

1 Corinthians 13:4–8 (NIV)

As we walk together, He teaches us how love takes time and how His time is infinite, more than our finite minds can even conceive. God shows us how His love is kind. He shows us people steeped in worldly riches and gently nudges our hearts to release envy because envy is not love. He shares unimaginable gifts with us and says, "Do not boast. It is by My Spirit, with My love. Be not proud for it is by My stripes that you are healed." His love comes in the minute you concede to it, and you cannot conceive of all the glorious riches it will bring to you.

When we misstep and judge others, He softly reminds us that His love is not rude. When we huddle up in the corner with a bad mindset and waste the day away, He quietly says, "Now go use My Word to save a soul. My love is not self-seeking."

When frustration turns to anger, and we want to yell, He helps us to see that His love is not easily angered. He tells us that love keeps no record of wrong and reminds us that our own trespasses have been forgiven.

"Love does not delight in evil but rejoices with the truth" (1 Corinthians 13:6, NIV). This verse is very real to me. My Jesus fought for me. I weep over the endurance of his faith. God tells us His love, "always protects, always trusts, always hopes, always perseveres" (1 Corinthians 13:7, NIV). When I think of all God and my Jesus have done for me, I understand that His "Love never fails" (1 Corinthians 13:8, NIV).

Let us adhere to the exact methods and habits we need to stay healthy forever. If we protect the hard-fought healing we have received, we can do our part to help heal everyone who crosses our path on our stairway to heaven. The true purpose of God's healing is for us to forgive and love one another, guiding each other in unity towards Christ's likeness.

We may stumble occasionally, but His love keeps us treading upward, not tripping downward. We flow in His love as we grow in into His likeness. Our healing is to reside on the peaks of His love during the valleys of our lives.

He restores my soul. He guides me in paths of righteousness for His name's sake. Even though I walk through the valley of the shadow of death, I will fear no evil, for You are with me; Your rod and Your staff, they comfort me. You prepare a table before me in the presence of my enemies. You anoint my head with oil; my cup overflows (Psalm 23:3–5).

A New Look Back

Now that we have moved closer to God, we can better sense the pain of others and pray for them in love, for the spark is in them. God created them, and He placed His love there. We can accept with faith that our journey in Him is always upward, regardless of what we feel. We will praise Him and rejoice because our position in Him is a purposeful and necessary part of His Kingdom.

Once we resolve, in our newfound freedom, the fact that even our failures are nothing more than valleys. Satan's favorite trick is to make us believe we are capable of stepping out of God's love. We are not going to listen to his lies.

If we have been sealed in the Holy Spirit (see Ephesians 1:13) and are seeking Him, we are irrevocably in His love.

The valley is where transformational work occurs. We grow and change when opposition is the strongest. If you feel weak, let me promise you that stepping back to where you came from will not help. That place has not changed. What has changed is you. You have left your past powerless over you by stepping out of Egypt. That place is still no good. The musty smell hovers, and its occupants still breathe the wrong air for the wrong reasons.

Remember what 1 Corinthians 15:33 (NIV) says, "Bad company corrupts good character."

Stepping up in the Valley

We are either in a valley of pain or a valley of the Lord's rebuke. If you have slipped back into sin or have stepped into new sin, you will soon find yourself in a valley. Step out of it by starting over with the stairs as quickly as possible.

Sometimes, you will feel that all is well, yet you feel down and out and cannot put your finger on the reason. When opposition is the strongest, you are usually at your weakest. Your awareness of His strength is imperative during this type of transition. This may be a valley of refinement, or as I like to call it, the Lord's training camp. Love God and keep stepping for Him in this life to attain your crown that is awaiting you in heaven.

The hardest thing I had to accept was the fact that I will always be in need of God's healing, regardless of how much I have healed. That is the absolute truth. Our consistent need for His love is a flame that we need to keep ablaze within us. That is why this book is not just about the steps to healing; it is also about the steps to staying healed.

A visual I like to picture is of a huge mountain range like the Alps. Imagine a beginning point at the very bottom, at sea level. As you begin to climb, you take some upward and some downward steps, but your trajectory is consistently upward. There are little valleys nestled between the peaks along the way. Even when you find yourself in a valley, you are still well above sea level.

Remembering taking a trip to Atlanta, where I traveled up into the Appalachian Mountains. You could feel the gradual climb as the topography and climate changed. When I arrived at my mother's home up on the stunning crest of a hill, I stepped out of the car. I felt the slope of the ground and steadied my balance as I acclimated to the land. The trip up had been beautiful, and in my mind, I had a picture of where we were on this grand mountainside.

When I left, I drove out of town taking the opposite direction. I went into the mountains instead of out. Traveling, I had to rethink my mountainside position. As I turned the corner off the road, leaving my mother's home, I saw a beautiful valley full of water. My eyes felt glazed over as my mind raced to try to catch all of the unexpected treasures. I was amazed at how God had scooped out a bowl on the tippy top of this huge peak and filled it with water.

I continued looking around and realized that as I consistently gained altitude, I took amazing dips and dives into little valleys and gorges along the way. The valleys and gorges only made the trip more interesting and adventurous! Make sure your valleys are God's enhancements, not sin traps, and remain in Him regardless of your natural circumstances.

I want to touch on the hard times in healing because they do happen, and I do not want anyone to feel they are alone in this challenge. Being healed and healing is a powerful place to be, but we are still human and will always have struggles. I want you to know that what you have accomplished in Christ is mighty. We can only get mightier as we step up, even when we pass through a valley.

In the valley, we will submit to God, resist the devil, and he will flee (James 4:7). His departure is not always as swift as we would like, but in the waiting period called perseverance, God makes us better. Sometimes, all we can do is stand on His Word, believe for truth, and wait. We do not give up or give in to our emotions.

Neither our devotion to Christ nor our efforts to follow Him are in vain. Paul wrote, "Hold out the word of life—in order that I may boast on the day of Christ that I did not run or labor for nothing" (Philippians 2:16, NIV). We ready our feet to step up regardless of our feelings; we step as soon as He gives permission to proceed.

We will dip and dive from the valley to the mountain peak. Do not let satan get a hold of you and make you think that God's refinement is punishment. Even if you have stumbled, you are not going to the bottom. God's love is unfailing. He is so perfect, and we are so imperfect that we must accept a life of consistent and necessary improvement in Him. First John 4:18 (NIV) tells us, "There is no fear in love. But perfect love drives out fear, because fear has to do with punishment. The one who fears is not made perfect in love."

At times, we are on a hard, cold, seemingly lonely road. My treatment, my separation, my divorce, and my dark nights were all valleys, but once I reached the next peak, a new blessing would appear. A beautiful, wonderful new blessing. His thoughts are so much higher! My husband Sam is one of those blessings, and he was a perfect, blatant answer to so many years of prayer. God is listening to you. He hears you. Please trust me! From our successful journey, we know by faith exactly what to do to endure. We use our tried and true stairs, new levels of awareness, and prayer. By the Spirit and through the Word, we will win.

We have just emerged from the valley, my sweet mask remover. Remember not to reside in your emotions but to reside in His love, always. Now step out onto the peak of His love and praise Him for your life restored and your purpose exposed. Our journey has been tough but rewarding; we know what to avoid and what to establish in our lives. Now we will rest for a while up on the tallest, highest peak of His love.

Standing Still on the Peaks

"Those who trust in the Lord are like Mount Zion, which cannot be shaken but endures forever. As the mountains surround Jerusalem, so the Lord surrounds his people both now and forevermore" (Psalm 125:1–2, NIV).

Psalm 125 is a song for pilgrims ascending to Jerusalem. Sojourning is exactly what we are doing; we are consistently ascending unto the temple of the heavenly Jerusalem.

My healed and healing friend in Christ with Christ in you, look how far you have climbed! You are described in Revelation 12:11 (KJV): "And they overcame him by the blood of the Lamb, and by the word of their testimony; and they loved not their lives unto the death." He shared with you all His pain; He wants you to share yours with others as He leads.

To me, functioning in God's love is the epitome of a healthy life. It just happens to be our last awareness. Why is the step and the action the same? Because everything cumulates in love, the very reason God sent His Son to heal us:

> *[God] made us alive with Christ even when we were dead in transgressions—it is by grace you have been saved. And God raised us up with Christ and seated us with Him in the heavenly realms in Christ Jesus, in order that in the coming ages He might show the incomparable riches of His grace, expressed in His kindness to us in Christ Jesus.*

> Ephesians 2:5–7 (NIV)

God has authorized us to be on these steps. With much authority comes much responsibility: in one word, our responsibility is love.

Satan wants us to believe that it would be arrogant of us to assume God's power. Society wants us to follow its controlling pharaoh-like powers. Scripture clearly states that God's power goes opposite to the world's. His authority is ours by grace, and the activation of that authority is seeded in the transference of His love (2 Corinthians 10).

Stepping in His love leads only to glory. When we fail to reside in His love, the scepter of our power lies inactive. We cannot escape God's love. His love is omnipresent and omnipotent. However, we can step out from under His blessing, power, anointing, honor, and authority if we are not in total surrender to His love.

As we have stepped through healing, we realize that the remedy for all our pain is God's perfect love. We call on lots of things for help, but when you discover the real thing, you realize that nothing else will do. God sacrificing His Son is a love we cannot comprehend. We feel that magnificent love in our healthy life, and since we are imperfect, we will forever seek more of His agape love. "Let all that I am praise the Lord;

with my whole heart, I will praise His holy name" (Psalm 103:1, NLT).

We can be saved, infilled to fullness, and activated in every office with every gift, but if we are not aware of how much God loves us, all of it is still tainted. His love bought you with a price. You are His, and He created you. You are so precious to Him. He wants to bestow a crown of worth on you that no man can remove. Let Him place a crown of His everlasting, indestructible, and undeniable love on your head, power from on high. He really, really loves you. His amazing love covers you and keeps you healthy.

Keep Climbing

Our eyes land on the gentle current flowing through the river in the base of the valley. We know that there is climbing involved, but He tells us His love will carry us the whole journey. The low, rolling hills cradling the river blend softly away, graduating as they rise into jagged mountain peaks. We realize that we are much higher than we expected because He exceeds our expectations. We are resting on the peaks of His love now, and we know our passage has been and is being blessed.

You have decided to put Him first, and in making that decision, you have subjected yourself to a love that will supersede the lowest valley by countering it with the highest peak.

Those who accept My commandments and obey them are the ones who love Me. And because they love Me, My Father will love them. And I will love them and reveal Myself to each of them (John 14:21, NLT).

Just as Job learned during his pain and trials, you will see in abundance your hurt counterbalanced in the blessing of where you are going.

God's peaks are endless because He has abundant wisdom and blessings for us to attain. We will travel through our valleys with the reminder of His peaks in our hearts and His love as a current to guide our steps. When we arrive in the valley, we will picture stairs leading us up out of the canyon; we will begin to climb with hope and faith, knowing the assent is never easy but always blessed.

Now we see but a poor reflection as in a mirror; then we shall see face to face. Now I know in part; then I shall know fully, even as I am fully known.

And now these three remain: faith, hope, and love. But the greatest of these is love (1 Corinthians 13:12–13).

The greatest is love because once we arrive with Him in heaven, we will have no need for faith or hope since He is love. Love will remain eternally.

He loves you more than any words I can say. Please know His love. Step into His love and then step up, up, up in faith. One day, we will smile from the mountain peak in the heavenly Jerusalem, and all our pain will subside. In the meantime, may these steps guide you to the power of His glorious, loving gift of heaven on earth, ascending until we meet on the peaks of His glory.

Love is patient; love is kind. It does not envy, it does not boast, it is not proud. It is not rude, it is not self-seeking, it is not easily angered, it keeps no record of wrongs. Love does not delight in evil but rejoices with the truth. It always protects, always trusts, always hopes, and always perseveres. Love never fails (1 Corinthians 13:4–8).

Congratulations, you have successfully made it up to the temple and into His Holy of Holies. You understand how to stand firm in the valley seasons of life and soak up the blessings on the peaks of His love. You are ready to share as God leads while you reside in His agape love. You have His love and have successfully added thirteen new levels of awareness and thirteen actions to your day! Do not forget to step up in Him forever.

But the eyes of the Lord are on those who fear Him, on those whose hope is in His unfailing love... (Psalm 33:18, emphasis added)

APPENDIX A

READ THE BIBLE IN ONE YEAR

Sep 1: Gen 1–3

Sep 2: Gen 4–7

Sep 3: Gen 8–11

Sep 4: Gen 12–15

Sep 5: Gen 16–18

Sep 6: Gen 19–21

Sep 7: Gen 22–24

Sep 8: Gen 25–26

Sep 9: Gen 27–29

Sep 10: Gen 30–31

Sep 11: Gen 32–34

Sep 12: Gen 35–37

Sep 13: Gen 38–40

Sep 14: Gen 41–42

Sep 15: Gen 43–45

Sep 16: Gen 46–47

Sep 17: Gen 48–50

Sep 18: Exod 1–3

Sep 19: Exod 4–6

Sep 20: Exod 7–9

Sep 21: Exod 10–12

Sep 22: Exod 13–15

Sep 23: Exod 16–18

Sep 24: Exod 19–21

Sep 25: Exod 22–24

Sep 26: Exod 25–27

Sep 27: Exod 28–29

Sep 28: Exod 30–32

Sep 29: Exod 33–35

Sep 30: Exod 36–38

Oct 1: Exod 39–40
Oct 2: Lev 1–4
Oct 3: Lev 5–7
Oct 4: Lev 8–10
Oct 5: Lev 11–13
Oct 6: Lev 14–15
Oct 7: Lev 16–18
Oct 8: Lev 19–21
Oct 9: Lev 22–23
Oct 10: Lev 24–25
Oct 11: Lev 26–27
Oct 12: Num 1–2
Oct 13: Num 3–4
Oct 14: Num 5–6
Oct 15: Num 7
Oct 16: Num 8–10
Oct 17: Num 11–13
Oct 18: Num 14–15
Oct 19: Num 16–17
Oct 20: Num 18–20
Oct 21: Num 21–22
Oct 22: Num 23–25
Oct 23: Num 26–27
Oct 24: Num 28–30
Oct 25: Num 31–32
Oct 26: Num 33–34
Oct 27: Num 35–36
Oct 28: Deut 1–2
Oct 29: Deut 3–4
Oct 30: Deut 5–7
Oct 31: Deut 8–10
Nov 1: Deut 11–13
Nov 2: Deut 14–16
Nov 3: Deut 17–20

Nov 4: Deut 21–23

Nov 5: Deut 24–27

Nov 6: Deut 28–29

Nov 7: Deut 30–31

Nov 8: Deut 32–34

Nov 9: Josh 1–4

Nov 10: Josh 5–8

Nov 11: Josh 9–11

Nov 12: Josh 12–15

Nov 13: Josh 16–18

Nov 14: Josh 19–21

Nov 15: Josh 22–24

Nov 16: Judg 1–2

Nov 17: Judg 3–5

Nov 18: Judg 6–7

Nov 19: Judg 8–9

Nov 20: Judg 10–12

Nov 21: Judg 13–15

Nov 22: Judg 16–18

Nov 23: Judg 19–21

Nov 24: Ruth 1–4

Nov 25: 1 Sam 1–3

Nov 26: 1 Sam 4–8

Nov 27: 1 Sam 9–12

Nov 28: 1 Sam 13–14

Nov 29: 1 Sam 15–17

Nov 30: 1 Sam 18–20

Dec 1: 1 Sam 21–24

Dec 2: 1 Sam 25–27

Dec 3: 1 Sam 28–31

Dec 4: 2 Sam 1–3

Dec 5: 2 Sam 4–7

Dec 6: 2 Sam 8–12

Dec 7: 2 Sam 13–15

Dec 8: 2 Sam 16–18
Dec 9: 2 Sam 19–21
Dec 10: 2 Sam 22–24
Dec 11: 1 Kings 1–2
Dec 12: 1 Kings 3–5
Dec 13: 1 Kings 6–7
Dec 14: 1 Kings 8–9
Dec 15: 1 Kings 10–11
Dec 16: 1 Kings 12–14
Dec 17: 1 Kings 15–17
Dec 18: 1 Kings 18–20
Dec 19: 1 Kings 21–22
Dec 20: 2 Kings 1–3
Dec 21: 2 Kings 4–5
Dec 22: 2 Kings 6–8
Dec 23: 2 Kings 9–11
Dec 24: 2 Kings 12–14
Dec 25: 2 Kings 15–17
Dec 26: 2 Kings 18–19
Dec 27: 2 Kings 20–22
Dec 28: 2 Kings 23–25
Dec 29: 1 Chron 1–2
Dec 30: 1 Chron 3–5
Dec 31: 1 Chron 6
Jan 1: 1 Chron 7–8
Jan 2: 1 Chron 9–11
Jan 3: 1 Chron 12–14
Jan 4: 1 Chron 15–17
Jan 5: 1 Chron 18–21
Jan 6: 1 Chron 22–24
Jan 7: 1 Chron 25–27
Jan 8: 1/2 Chron 28/1
Jan 9: 2 Chron 2–5
Jan 10: 2 Chron 6–8

Jan 11: 2 Chron 9–12

Jan 12: 2 Chron 13–17

Jan 13: 2 Chron 18–20

Jan 14: 2 Chron 21–24

Jan 15: 2 Chron 25–27

Jan 16: 2 Chron 28–31

Jan 17: 2 Chron 32–34

Jan 18: 2 Chron 35–36

Jan 19: Ezra 1–3

Jan 20: Ezra 4–7

Jan 21: Ezra 8–10

Jan 22: Neh 1–3

Jan 23: Neh 4–6

Jan 24: Neh 7

Jan 25: Neh 8–9

Jan 26: Neh 10–11

Jan 27: Neh 12–13

Jan 28: Est 1–5

Jan 29: Esther 6–10

Jan 30: Job 1–4

Jan 31: Job 5–7

Feb 1: Job 8–10

Feb 2: Job 11–13

Feb 3: Job 14–16

Feb 4: Job 17–20

Feb 5: Job 21–23

Feb 6: Job 24–28

Feb 7: Job 29–31

Feb 8: Job 32–34

Feb 9: Job 35–37

Feb 10: Job 38–39

Feb 11: Job 40–42

Feb 12: Ps 1–8

Feb 13: Ps 9–16

Feb 14: Ps 17–20
Feb 15: Ps 21–25
Feb 16: Ps 26–31
Feb 17: Ps 32–35
Feb 18: Ps 36–39
Feb 19: Ps 40–45
Feb 20: Ps 46–50
Feb 21: Ps 51–57
Feb 22: Ps 58–65
Feb 23: Ps 66–69
Feb 24: Ps 70–73
Feb 25: Ps 74–77
Feb 26: Ps 78–79
Feb 27: Ps 80–85
Feb 28/29: Ps 86–89
Mar 1: Ps 90–95
Mar 2: Ps 96–102
Mar 3: Ps 103–105
Mar 4: Ps 106–107
Mar 5: Ps 108–114
Mar 6: Ps 115–118
Mar 7: Ps 119:1–88
Mar 8: Ps 119:89–176
Mar 9: Ps 120–132
Mar 10: Ps 133–139
Mar 11: Ps 140–145
Mar 12: Ps 146–150
Mar 13: Prov 1–3
Mar 14: Prov 4–6
Mar 15: Prov 7–9
Mar 16: Prov 10–12
Mar 17: Prov 13–15
Mar 18: Prov 16–18
Mar 19: Prov 19–21

Mar 20: Prov 22–23
Mar 21: Prov 24–26
Mar 22: Prov 27–29
Mar 23: Prov 30–31
Mar 24: Eccles 1–4
Mar 25: Eccles 5–8
Mar 26: Eccles 9–12
Mar 27: Solomon 1–8
Mar 28: Isa 1–4
Mar 29: Isa 5–8
Mar 30: Isa 9–12
Mar 31: Isa 13–17
Apr 1: Isa 18–22
Apr 2: Isa 23–27
Apr 3: Isa 28–30
Apr 4: Isa 31–35
Apr 5: Isa 36–41
Apr 6: Isa 42–44
Apr 7: Isa 45–48
Apr 8: Isa 49–53
Apr 9: Isa 54–58
Apr 10: Isa 59–63
Apr 11: Isa 64–66
Apr 12: Jer 1–3
Apr 13: Jer 4–6
Apr 14: Jer 7–9
Apr 15: Jer 10–13
Apr 16: Jer 14–17
Apr 17: Jer 18–22
Apr 18: Jer 23–25
Apr 19: Jer 26–29
Apr 20: Jer 30–31
Apr 21: Jer 32–34
Apr 22: Jer 35–37

Apr 23: Jer 38–41

Apr 24: Jer 42–45

Apr 25: Jer 46–48

Apr 26: Jer 49–50

Apr 27: Jer 51–52

Apr 28: Lam 1–3:36

Apr 29: Lam 3:37–5:22

Apr 30: Ezek 1–4

May 1: Ezek 5–8

May 2: Ezek 9–12

May 3: Ezek 13–15

May 4: Ezek 16–17

May 5: Ezek 18–20

May 6: Ezek 21–22

May 7: Ezek 23–24

May 8: Ezek 25–27

May 9: Ezek 28–30

May 10: Ezek 31–33

May 11: Ezek 34–36

May 12: Ezek 37–39

May 13: Ezek 40–42

May 14: Ezek 43–45

May 15: Ezek 46–48

May 16: Dan 1–3

May 17: Dan 4–6

May 18: Dan 7–9

May 19: Dan 10–12

May 20: Hos 1–7

May 21: Hos 8–14

May 22: Joel 1–3

May 23: Amos 1–5

May 24: Amos 6–9

May 25: Obad–Jonah

May 26: Mic 1–7

The Maskquerade

May 27: Nah 1–3
May 28: Hab–Zeph
May 29: Hag 1–2
May 30: Zech 1–7
May 31: Zech 8–14
Jun 1: Mal 1–4
Jun 2: Matt 1–4
Jun 3: Matt 5–6
Jun 4: Matt 7–8
Jun 5: Matt 9–10
Jun 6: Matt 11–12
Jun 7: Matt 13–14
Jun 8: Matt 15–17
Jun 9: Matt 18–19
Jun 10: Matt 20–21
Jun 11: Matt 22–23
Jun 12: Matt 24–25
Jun 13: Matt 26
Jun 14: Matt 27–28
Jun 15: Mark 1–3
Jun 16: Mark 4–5
Jun 17: Mark 6–7
Jun 18: Mark 8–9
Jun 19: Mark 10–11
Jun 20: Mark 12–13
Jun 21: Mark 14
Jun 22: Mark 15–16
Jun 23: Luke 1
Jun 24: Luke 2–3
Jun 25: Luke 4–5
Jun 26: Luke 6–7
Jun 27: Luke 8–9
Jun 28: Luke 10–11
Jun 29: Luke 12–13

Jun 30: Luke 14–16

Jul 1: Luke 17–18

Jul 2: Luke 19–20

Jul 3: Luke 21–22

Jul 4: Luke 23–24

Jul 5: John 1–2

Jul 6: John 3–4

Jul 7: John 5–6

Jul 8: John 7–8

Jul 9: John 9–10

Jul 10: John 11–12

Jul 11: John 13–15

Jul 12: John 16–18

Jul 13: John 19–21

Jul 14: Acts 1–3

Jul 15: Acts 4–6

Jul 16: Acts 7–8

Jul 17: Acts 9–10

Jul 18: Acts 11–13

Jul 19: Acts 14–15

Jul 20: Acts 16–17

Jul 21: Acts 18–20

Jul 22: Acts 21–23

Jul 23: Acts 24–26

Jul 24: Acts 27–28

Jul 25: Rom 1–3

Jul 26: Rom 4–7

Jul 27: Rom 8–10

Jul 28: Rom 11–13

Jul 29: Rom 14–16

Jul 30: 1 Cor 1–4

Jul 31: 1 Cor 5–8

Aug 1: 1 Cor 9–11

Aug 2: 1 Cor 12–14

Aug 3: 1 Cor 15–16
Aug 4: 2 Cor 1–4
Aug 5: 2 Cor 5–9
Aug 6: 2 Cor 10–13
Aug 7: Gal 1–3
Aug 8: Gal 4–6
Aug 9: Eph 1–3
Aug 10: Eph 4–6
Aug 11: Phil 1–4
Aug 12: Col 1–4
Aug 13: 1 Thess 1–5
Aug 14: 2 Thess 1–3
Aug 15: 1 Tim 1–6
Aug 16: 2 Tim 1–4
Aug 17: Titus–Philem
Aug 18: Heb 1–6
Aug 19: Heb 7–10
Aug 20: Heb 11–13
Aug 21: James 1–5
Aug 22: 1 Pet 1–5
Aug 23: 2 Pet 1–3
Aug 24: 1 John 1–5
Aug 25: 2 John–Jude
Aug 26: Rev 1–3
Aug 27: Rev 4–8
Aug 28: Rev 9–12
Aug 29: Rev 13–16
Aug 30: Rev 17–19
Aug 31: Rev 20–22

Printed in the USA
CPSIA information can be obtained
at www.ICGtesting.com
LVHW010924151024
793857LV00013B/583

9 798893 336061